THE AMERICAN WILDERNESS AND ITS FUTURE

CONSERVATION VERSUS USE

THE AMERICAN WILDERNESS AND ITS FUTURE

CONSERVATION VERSUS USE

EDWARD F. DOLAN

Franklin Watts
New York London Toronto Sydney

Map and diagram by Vantage Art, Inc.

Photographs copyright © : Photo Researchers, Inc.: frontis (Jen & Des Bartlett), insert pp. 3 bottom (Richard Parker), 5, 9 bottom (both Farrell Grehan), 6, 10 (both Keith Gunnar), 8 bottom (Max & Kit Hunn), 9 top (George Dineen), 14 (Tim Davis), 16 (Steve Kraseman); The Bettmann Archive: pp. 1, 2, 7; UPI/Bettmann Newsphotos: pp. 3 top, 8 top, 13; Reuters/Bettmann Newsphotos: p. 15; Woodfin Camp & Assoc./Jonathan Blair: p. 4; New York Public Library, Picture Collection: pp. 11, 12.

Library of Congress Cataloging-in-Publication Data

Dolan, Edward F., 1924–
The American wilderness and its future : conservation versus use / Edward F. Dolan.
p. cm.
Includes bibliographical references (p.) and index.
Summary: Describes the conflict between environmentalists and commercial and recreational interests over how the remaining wilderness areas in America should be used.
ISBN 0-531-11062-1
1. National parks and reserves—United States—Juvenile literature. 2. Forest reserves—United States—Juvenile literature. 4. Public lands—United States—Juvenile literature. 5. Conservation of natural resources—United States—Juvenile literature. 6. Natural resources—United States—Juvenile literature. 7. Environmental policy—United States—Juvenile literature. [1. Wilderness areas. 2. National parks and reserves. 3. Conservation of natural resources.] I. Title.
SB482.A4D65 1992

333.78′2′160973—dc20 91-33440 CIP AC

Printed in the United States of America
5 4 3 2 1

CONTENTS

ACKNOWLEDGMENTS

For kindly providing me with basic research materials and for answering specific questions in the preparation of this book, I wish to express my appreciation to the Forest Service of the United States Department of Agriculture; the National Park Service of the United States Department of the Interior; Robert H. Nelson of the Office of Program Analysis, the United States Department of the Interior; The Wildlife Society; Jan Bedrosian, public affairs specialist, California state office, U.S. Bureau of Land Management; and the offices of Senator Alan Cranston (California) and Congresspersons Barbara Boxer (California), Wayne Owens (Utah), and Barbara Vucanovich (Nevada). My special thanks to Janet Allen of Congresswoman Boxer's office for her assistance and to John D. de Golia for his helpful editorial comments and suggestions.

A wilderness, in contrast with those areas where man and his own works dominate the landscape, is hereby recognized as an area where the earth and its community of life are untrammeled by man, where man himself is a visitor that does not remain.

—*The Wilderness Act*,
established by the
United States Congress,
September, 1963

1
THE BATTLEGROUND

It is a day of brilliant sunshine. You and your family have driven hundreds of miles to visit the giant canyon, one of the scenic wonders in the United States. Now you stand at its edge and peer downward. But you can barely see the steep, vast walls of fantastically colored rock that rise from its depths. Nor can you see the river that pulses along its floor almost a mile below your feet. The walls and the river are hidden beneath a layer of yellow-gray smog—a smog caused in part by the thousands of vehicles that have come to the canyon edge this day. The smog is also caused in greater part by the smoke from a nearby coal-burning electric power plant and by polluted air flowing in from distant Los Angeles in California.

It is another day of brilliant sunshine, but also a day of latticework shadows as you and your family drive through a forest on the Pacific Coast. All around you are Douglas firs—majestic trees that seem to rise beyond their typically 150 to 210-foot heights and thrust their boughs deep into the sky. From time to time, great big trucks coming in the opposite direction roar past you. Chained to their flatbeds are the trunks of trees that are headed for nearby mills to be sliced into millions of board feet of timber. Your parents say they have heard that the logging industry is stripping the forest of some of the oldest and finest trees in the nation.

Now you and your parents are vacationing in the southeastern United States. You have come to see the country's premier wetland—an expanse covering almost 1.4 million acres of water-drenched land and mangrove forests that serves as the home and breeding grounds for countless birds and other animals. But you soon discover that the water of the wetland is fast disappearing. Much of the water is being drained away to serve nearby cities and industries. The result: a frightening percentage of the area's wildlife is dying.

You encounter these three experiences while traveling in the vast American wilderness. The first occurs on a visit to the Grand Canyon National Park in Arizona, the second on a drive through Washington State's sprawling Olympic National Forest, and the third on a trip to the Everglades National Park in Florida. The environmental destruction you've seen—the smog, the felled trees chained to logging trucks, and the loss of plant and animal life—are symptoms of the problems that besiege much of the nation's wilderness today. These and other problems are turning the American wilderness into a battleground between environmentalists and commercial and recreational interests over how it should be treated now and in the future.

Hundreds of millions of acres make up the American wilderness. They present us with every type of scenery imaginable—from forested mountains and valleys to rivers, lakes, marshy wetlands, windswept deserts, rolling plains, and, alongside our oceans, sandy and rocky coastlines.

Who owns and holds responsibility for all these acres? Vast tracts of land, such as the three you've visited in this book, are owned by the federal government; they are public lands that belong to all United States citizens. Equally vast tracts of public lands are owned by the states, by counties within the states, and by local communities. Still others are privately owned by individuals, families, and commercial concerns such as logging and mining companies. Regardless of their ownership, they have one thing in common. They are all part of the battleground.

THE CONFLICT

To understand the controversy that has turned our wilderness into a battleground, we need to begin with two basic facts. Both apply to the public lands held by the U.S. federal government.

> *Some lands originally were set aside by the government so that these magnificent outdoor settings could be protected from commercial development and preserved for the use of anyone seeking the pleasure and spiritual refreshment found in such outdoor activities as camping and sight-seeing.*
>
> *Most lands were designated for "multiple use," meaning that they could be employed for a variety of recreational purposes—not only camping and sight-seeing but also hunting, skiing, fishing, and today's off-road driving and racing—and for commercial purposes, such as logging, mining, oil drilling, and grazing.*

How did the conflict arise? First, many of the lands set aside for our enjoyment—especially our national parks—today have problems that threaten to destroy their beauty and defeat their very purpose. Such lands are being overwhelmed by an increasing flood of visitors and chronic traffic gridlock. Some have become victims of air pollution and acid rain that, although originating elsewhere and carried to them on the winds, are harming and killing the wildlife. These and other problems have triggered a debate over what can be done to preserve the beauty of the park settings while allowing visitors to continue to enjoy them.

Another growing concern is that many visitors are pursuing hobbies injurious to several wilderness regions. The environmentalists blame visitors who race such off-road vehicles as dirt bikes, dune buggies, and Jeeps over the lands, particularly those in the desert and seashore areas. These visitors are accused of desecrating the lands themselves, their plant and animal life, and, in some instances, the historical sites and artifacts found on these lands. Many people are urging that all such activities be banned, while the riders and drivers angrily insist that, as taxpayers, they too are paying for the support of the lands and thus have a right to pursue their hobbies on them.

Next, there is a growing concern that the commercial activities—logging and mining, for instance—permitted on certain federal lands are harming them beyond repair. Logging has become the target of the most attention and anger, with environmentalists and their supporters claiming that the logging industry is savagely hacking away at some of the nation's most precious timberland and, in doing so, is destroying countless species of plant and animal life. Using the Olympic National Forest in the state of Washington as an example of the harm being done (only 90,000 of its original 600,000 acres remain uncut),[1] environmentalists are demanding that logging be curtailed and, in some areas, stopped altogether. For its part, the lumber industry contends that the logging provides thousands of families with livelihoods, as well as supplies the nation and the world with the material required for a wide variety of needed products that range from homes and buildings to furniture and paper.

This is but a brief picture of the conflict being waged on the federal lands. But what of the state and privately owned areas? The state parks are also suffering problems of overcrowding and air pollution. And the outcry against such commercial activities as logging on some federal lands is also being leveled against similar pursuits on the state and privately owned lands.

THE BATTLEGROUND

Vast as the battleground is, we will visit many of its regions in this book—its forests, wetlands, rivers, lakes, coastlines, and deserts—and talk about the troubles faced by each. But two points should be kept in mind as we begin our trip.

First, most of our time will be spent in our country's forests, for it is there that the conflict is being waged at its fiercest. Second, we will deal mainly with the wilderness lands held by the federal government. This is because their problems are nationwide in scope and reflect those of the state and privately owned lands. But, as we go along, we will talk of the state and privately owned lands so that a full picture of the conflict is gained.

The federal government owns more than 500 million acres of wilderness. They are to be found not only throughout the United States but also in such U.S.–held territories as Puerto Rico, the Virgin Islands, and American Samoa.

The lands have been given various designations that are familiar to us all, such as national parks and national forests, and national wildlife refuges. The designation of a particular tract depends on a number of factors—for example, some of the lands are set aside for the preservation of their scenery, some for the preservation of their wildlife species, some for the prudent management of their resources (such as their mineral deposits), and some for the enjoyment of the public.

In all, however, the federal lands are divided into four categories, namely:

1. The lands within the National Park System;
2. The lands in the National Forest System;
3. The lands held by the U.S. Bureau of Land Management;
4. The complex of lands known variously as *Wilderness Areas* or simply as the *Wilderness.*

To avoid confusion with the general use of the word "wilderness" in this book, we will always refer to the lands in the fourth category as Wilderness Areas.

The National Park System

Some 80 million acres are assigned to the National Park System. They are divided into 355 public facilities, which are technically called *units.*[2] The units are found in forty-nine states, the District of Columbia, American Samoa, Guam, Puerto Rico, Saipan, and the Virgin Islands. Making up the units are:

- National parks
- Preserves
- Recreation areas
- Scenic trails
- Wild and scenic rivers and riverways
- Monuments
- Memorials
- Historical parks
- Historic sites
- Battlefields, battlefield parks
- Military parks
- Lakeshores and seashores
- Parkways

Also included in the system are the White House and its grounds.

The National Park Service of the Department of the Interior manages the system. The use of the system's lands for such commercial activities as logging, mining, and such is prohibited.

By far the greatest amount of acreage in the system is given over to four unit types—the national parks, preserves, monuments, and recreation areas.

National Parks. *Fifty areas, encompassing more than 47.3 million acres, have been set aside as national parks. A national park is customarily a large land or water tract that provides the public with a wide variety of activities and accommodations. Activities can range from sight-seeing to hiking and camping, while the accommodations can range from hotels and cabins to campsites for tents and recreational vehicles. The oldest national park is Yellowstone National Park. Established in 1872 and located in Wyoming, Montana, and Idaho, it covers upward of 2.2 million acres and offers visitors such diverse scenery as mountains, meadows, and lakes. It contains the world's greatest collection of geysers and hot springs, more than 10,000 in all. The best known of the geysers is the internationally famous Old Faithful.*

National Preserves. *Some 22.1 million acres are assigned to national preserves. These areas, fourteen in all, have been established primarily for the protection of their special and prized resources, among them their trees, minerals, fuels, and varieties of wildlife. Diverse outdoor activities are allowed in the preserves. Others, such as fishing and hunting, may be permitted in certain preserves if they do not threaten the natural resources there. Commercial activities, among them oil drilling,*

Figure 1. The National Park System

Isle Royale
Apostle Islands
Pictured Rocks
Sleeping Bear Dunes
WI
MI
Theodore Roosevelt's Inaugural
Effigy Mounds
Perry's Victory
James A. Garfield
Cuyahoga Valley
Herbert Hoover
Indiana Dunes
IL
IN
OH
Mound City Group
Lincoln Home
William Howard Taft
George Rogers Clark
Lincoln Boyhood
Abraham Lincoln Birthplace
KY
Mammoth Cave
Ozark
Fort Donelson
Buffalo
AR
Shiloh
Brices Cross Roads
Hot Springs
Tupelo
Natchez Trace Trail
MS
Vicksburg
Natchez
LA
Jean Lafitte
Gulf Islands
TN
Stones River
Obed
Cumberland Gap
Big South Fork
Carl Sandburg Home
Russell Cave
Kennesaw Mountain
AL
Horseshoe Bend
Tuskegee Institute
Chickamauga and Chattanooga
Chattahoochee River
Martin Luther King, Jr.
GA
Ocmulgee
Andersonville
Jimmy Carter
Ninety Six
Congaree Swamp
SC
Charles Pinckney
Fort Sumter
Fort Pulaski
Fort Frederica
Cumberland Island
Timucuan
Fort Caroline
Castillo de San Marcos
Fort Matanzes
Canaveral
FL
De Soto
Big Cypress
Everglades
Biscayne
Fort Jefferson
Andrew Johnson
Great Smoky Mountains
Kings Mountain
Cowpens
NC
Moores Creek
Cape Lookout
Guilford Courthouse
Blue Ridge Parkway
Booker T. Washington
VA
Appomattox Court House
Wright Brothers
Fort Raleigh
Cape Hatteras
Gauley River
New River Gorge
Bluestone
WV
Richmond
Petersburg
Maggie L. Walker
Colonial
Fredericksburg and Spotsylvania
Shenandoah
Prince William Forest
Thomas Stone
George Washington Birthplace
Assateague Island
Harpers Ferry
Manassas
Chesapeake and Ohio Canal
Friendship Hill
Antietam
Fort Necessity
Gettysburg
Hampton
Fort McHenry
Johnstown Flood
Allegheny Portage Railroad
Eisenhower
Hopewell Furnace
Valley Forge
PA
Delaware Water Gap
Steamtown
Delaware
Upper Delaware
Morristown
Edison
Edgar Allan Poe
Independence
Thaddeus Kosciuszko
Vanderbilt Mansion
Women's Rights
Martin Van Buren
Fort Stanwix
NY
Saratoga
Springfield Armory
Saint-Gaudens
Saugus Iron Works
Salem Maritime
VT NH
Lowell
MA
Appalachian Trail
ME
Saint Croix Island
Acadia
Adams
Boston
Boston African-American
Frederick Law Olmsted
John Fitzgerald Kennedy
Longfellow
Minute Man
Cape Cod
Roger Williams
Home of Franklin D. Roosevelt
Eleanor Roosevelt
Saint Paul's Church
Sagamore Hill
Fire Island
Castle Clinton
Federal Hall
Gateway
General Grant
Hamilton Grange
Statue of Liberty
Theodore Roosevelt Birthplace
Arlington House
Clara Barton
Constitution Gardens
Ford's Theatre
Fort Washington
Frederick Douglass
George Washington Parkway
Greenbelt
John F. Kennedy Center
Lincoln Memorial
Lyndon Baines Johnson
Monocacy
National Capital Parks
National Mall
Pennsylvania Avenue
Piscateway
Potomac Heritage Trail
Rock Creek
Theodore Roosevelt Island
Thomas Jefferson Memorial
Vietnam Veterans Memorial
Washington Monument
White House
Wolf Trap Farm
PUERTO RICO
and U.S. VIRGIN ISLANDS
San Juan
Virgin Islands
Buck Island Reef
Christiansted
USS Arizona Memorial
Kalaupapa
Haleakala
Puukohola Heiau
Kaloko-Honokohau
Pu'uhonua o Honaunau
Hawaii Volcanoes
HAWAII
GUAM
War in the Pacific

may also be permitted if they, too, do not unduly threaten the area's natural resources.

National Monuments. *There are seventy-nine national monuments in the United States. A monument is an area that has been set aside for the protection of one or more natural resources or wonders. For example, the Muir Woods National Monument of 553 California acres near San Francisco preserves and protects a stand of virgin coastal redwood trees. Some 4.8 million acres are devoted to national monuments.*

National Recreation Areas. *Eighteen sites serve as national recreation areas. They are customarily established in the vicinity of dams, reservoirs, or other water sources that make them ideal for such outdoor activities as swimming, boating, hiking, and picnicking. One of the best known is the Lake Mead Recreation Area in Nevada. Spreading over more than 26,700 acres, it came into being when Lakes Mead and Mohave were formed due to the construction of the Hoover and Davis dams on the Colorado River. More than 3.6 million acres are devoted to national recreation areas.*

The National Forest System

The National Forest System encompasses some 191 million acres and consists of 156 national forests and 19 national grasslands.[3] The system's lands lie in forty-four states, Puerto Rico, and the Virgin Islands, and are managed by the Forest Service of the U.S. Department of Agriculture.

For ease of management, the national forests are divided among nine regions, with each region named for its geographical location. The regions in the nation's West house the most forests. For example, the Pacific Northwest Region encompasses two states (Oregon and Washington) and boasts twenty-two forests. The Pacific Southwest Region (California and Hawaii) has twenty. The Northern Region (Idaho, Montana, and North Dakota) contains thirteen. Two are found in the Alaska Region, which covers that state alone.

As for the national grasslands, they are located in nine states—Wyoming, Colorado, New Mexico, Texas, Oklahoma, Kansas, Nebraska, and North and South Dakota.

The National Forest System offers a wide variety of outdoor activities to the visitor, among them camping, fishing, hiking, skiing, canoeing, and sight-seeing. The system features 108,381 miles of trails, 3,338 miles of rivers, more than 4,400 campgrounds, and upward of 1,400 picnic grounds.

According to the Department of Agriculture, the national forests and grasslands annually handle about 30 million visitor-days of hunting and fishing and some 17 million visitor-days of such activities as sight-seeing and nature study. The department computes a visitor-day as the equivalent of one person using a forest facility for twelve hours, twelve persons using a facility for one hour, or any equivalent combination.

Unlike the national parklands, however, the forests and grasslands are not reserved solely for the public's enjoyment. Under the "multiple-use" concept, portions of them are also employed for commercial purposes. Of the system's 191 million acres, 86.5 percent are classified as commercial timberlands. The Forest Service is empowered to lease the rights to log, mine, graze livestock, and drill for oil to commercial operations, with the revenues going to the federal government.

Lands Held by the U.S. Bureau of Land Management

The Bureau of Land Management was formed in 1946.[4] Its main job is to manage the commercial activities on federal lands in the nation's West that were not contained within national parks, forests, or wildlife refuges. Some

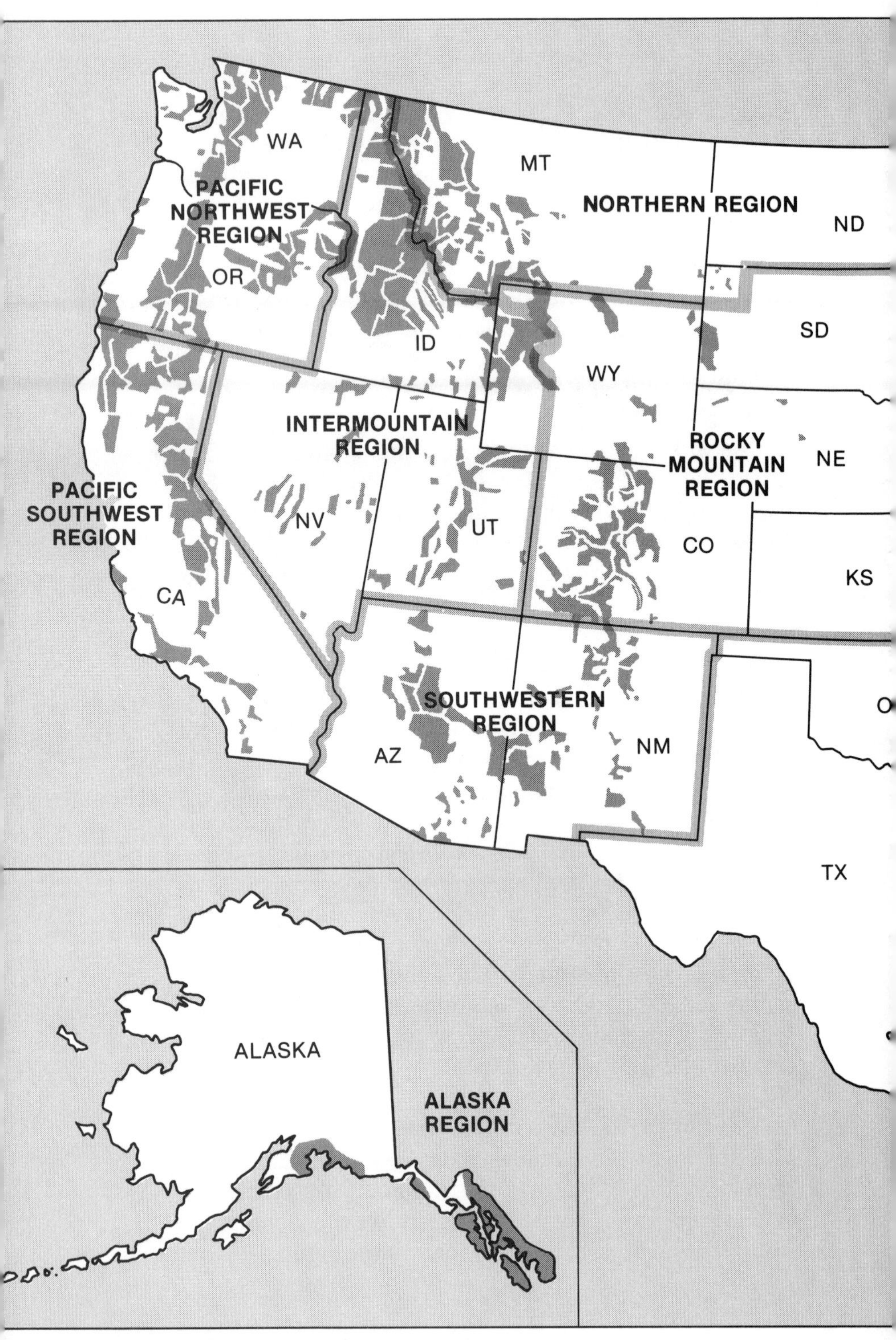

Figure 2. The National Forests

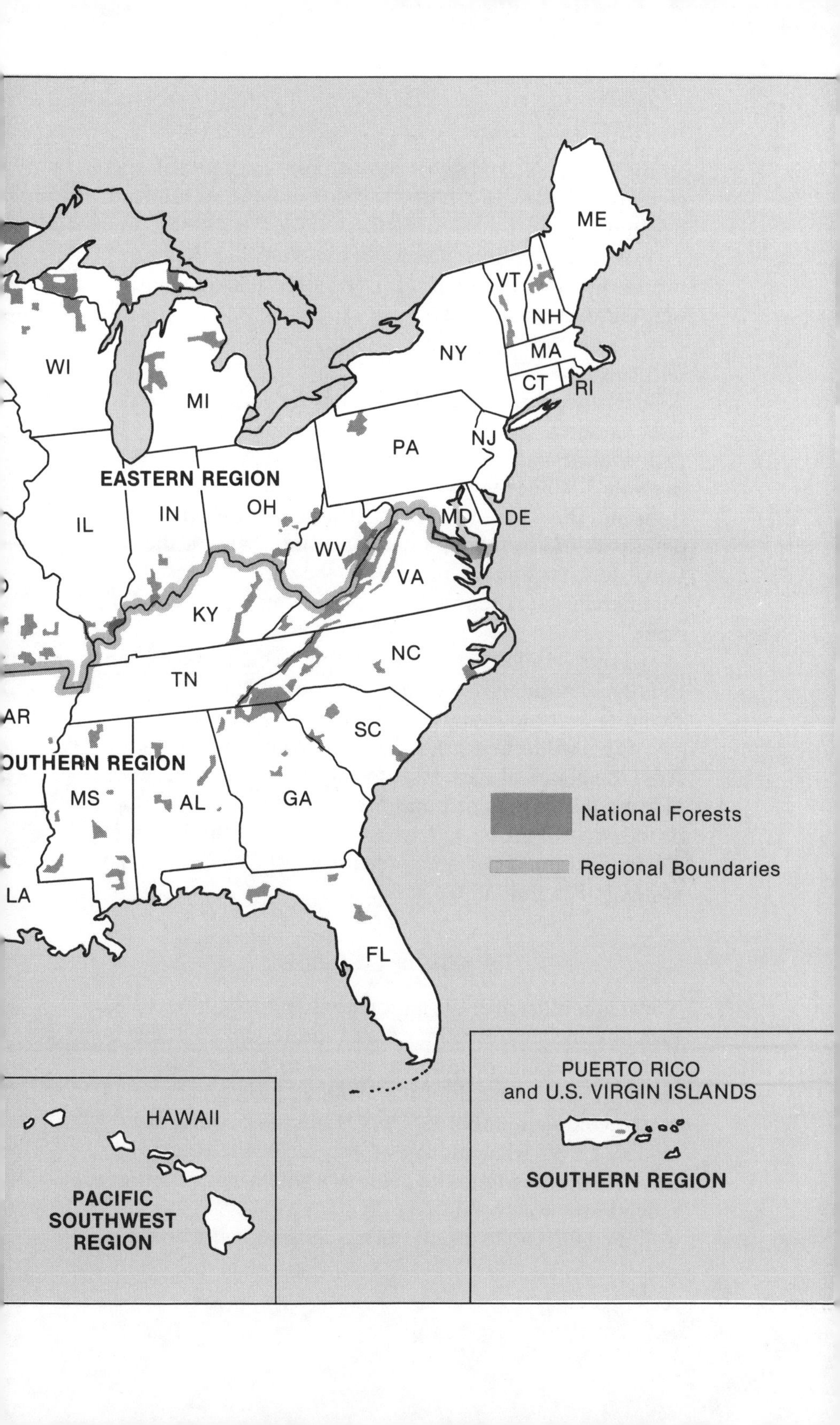
ME
VT
NH
MA
NY
CT
RI
WI
MI
PA
NJ
EASTERN REGION
IL
IN
OH
MD
DE
WV
VA
KY
NC
TN
AR
SC
OUTHERN REGION
MS
AL
GA
National Forests
Regional Boundaries
LA
FL
PUERTO RICO
and U.S. VIRGIN ISLANDS
HAWAII
SOUTHERN REGION
PACIFIC
SOUTHWEST
REGION

of the bureau's lands are put to both commercial and recreational uses. In all, about 250 million acres are held by the bureau.

As does the Forest Service, the BLM has the power to lease portions of its lands for commercial logging, grazing, and other activities.

Wilderness Areas

Wilderness areas are wild and remote regions that the U.S. Congress has set aside so that their natural resources and wildlife can be preserved in as pristine a state as possible.[5] While the areas are accessible for hiking and camping, they do not offer the roads and guest accommodations found in the national parks and many of the national forests. For the most part, they are not leased for commercial use, though livestock grazing is permitted in some areas.

Four hundred and seventy-four regions have been thus far designated as wilderness areas. They are to be found in forty-four states and cover 90.7 million acres.

The wilderness areas are not considered separate from the National Park and Forest systems and the lands held by the Bureau of Land Management. For example, of today's 474 areas, 329 are located within the National Forest System. They are spread over 32.1 million of the system's 191 million acres.

THE ROOTS OF THE CONFLICT

Today's conflict over the nation's wilderness can be traced back to the conservationist and preservationist movements of the nineteenth century. Both movements took shape in the latter half of the 1800s and were made up of a burgeoning number of Americans who were deeply troubled over what industry—especially the logging industry—was doing to the country's wilderness as settlers moved ever westward.

People tend to use the terms *conservationist, preserva-*

tionist, and *environmentalist* interchangeably, but each represents a distinct philosophy. The conservationists were interested in having the wilderness lands managed carefully and scientifically so that their resources could be wisely used for commercial benefits needed by the nation and would not be wasted. The preservationists wanted to see the nation's scenic wonders *completely* protected from commercial use. In many ways, the aims of the preservationists matched those of today's environmentalists. The principal difference between the two is one of scope. The preservationists were primarily concerned with keeping the land in its natural state while today's environmentalists are also concerned with environmental problems that did not exist in the late nineteenth century.

And what was the logging industry doing at the time the two movements took shape? To meet the growing demand for wood to build homes and buildings, it was following the settlers westward and leveling countless acres of woodland as it went. The demand for lumber had earlier denuded many of New England's forests. Now, in the nineteenth century, the industry had penetrated the southern states and Wisconsin, Minnesota, and Michigan. Before the century was over, more than 160 billion board feet of white pine would disappear from Michigan alone. No more than 6 billion board feet remained.

Both the conservationists and preservationists could see that the timber industry, if not checked, might well strip the entire country of one of its most valuable and beautiful resources. Each movement launched a campaign on behalf of the nation's wilderness lands. The preservationists, headed by the famous naturalist John Muir (whom we'll meet in chapter 2), urged the federal government to set aside some of the most breathtaking spots so that they could be safeguarded and preserved for the public's enjoyment for all time to come. The conservationists called for the government to undertake policies that would see the resources contained in the wilderness lands carefully managed and controlled so that they would not be lost to future generations.

Out of the two movements came the first of the millions of acres that today comprise the National Park and Forest systems—lands that are currently in the grip of a conflict that has turned them into vast battlegrounds. We turn now to the early history of that conflict as it was waged by the preservationists on the lands that in time became part of the National Park System.

2
OUR NATIONAL PARKS: THEIR STORY

In the early 1870s, a group of explorers came out of the Far West and arrived in Washington, D.C., with news of a magnificent expanse of land they had seen that stretched through parts of the Wyoming and Montana territories.[1] They spoke of its mountains, its meadows, its lakes, its streams and rivers, and its myriad hot springs and geysers. They told Congress that it should be made safe from the logging, mining, and farming activities that were altering much of the western landscape, and they urged Congress to set this land aside for the public's use and enjoyment.

The explorers were assisted in their plea by members of a U.S. Geological and Geographical Survey team that had recently worked in the region. Paintings and photographs produced by the team members so impressed the U.S. Congress that, on March 1, 1872, it enacted a bill that set the area aside as "a public park or pleasuring ground for the benefit and enjoyment of the people." Created that day was the country's first national park—Yellowstone National Park. Today, it occupies the northwest corner of the state of Wyoming, with some of its 2.2 million acres spilling into Idaho and Montana.

The founding of Yellowstone heartened the growing number of preservation-minded Americans and launched what was to become the country's National Park System. But it accomplished even more. Word of it spread to other nations that were also worried about their rural lands and inspired them to set aside regions for the use and enjoyment of their people. Today, the U.S. National Park System is reflected in similar systems in one hundred countries throughout the world. Those systems contain some 1,200 parks and other facilities.

Since 1872, the National Park System has grown to 355 public facilities that encompass approximately 80 million acres. The system owes much of its growth and expansion to a number of men and women and two acts of Congress.

One of the major figures—in the minds of many, *the* major figure—in the development of the system was the lanky and white-bearded naturalist and leader of the preservationist movement, John Muir. His work was of such importance that he is remembered today as "the Father of Our National Parks."

THE NATURALIST FROM SCOTLAND

The son of a storekeeper, John Muir was born in the town of Dunbar, Scotland, on April 21, 1838, and was brought to the United States by his family when he was eleven years old.[2] Wandering the fields around Dunbar as a boy, and later those surrounding his new home at Portage, Wisconsin, endowed him with a deep love of nature that was to give him his life's work.

Eager to study nature, Muir embarked on a long journey when he was in his twenties. The first leg of the trip took him on a 1,000-mile walk from Indianapolis, Indiana, to the Gulf of Mexico. All along the way, he stopped to scribble notes on and sketch pictures of the plant life he encountered. Then, on reaching the Gulf, he sailed to Cuba for a short stay. Next, he traveled on to California. There, at the end of a 150-mile, note-taking hike from San Francisco into the Sierra Nevada Mountains, he chanced upon the wondrous spot that would start him on his way to becoming "the Father of Our National Parks"—the Yosemite Valley.

Surrounded by the valley's giant granite walls that rose to heights of 3,000 to 4,000 feet, its breathtaking meadows and streams, its slender but magnificent waterfalls (one of their number being the highest in the United States), and the forests that spread away for miles into the circling mountains, Muir spent the next six years of his life at Yosemite. He studied the nature there and concluded that the valley had been formed, at least in part, by ancient glacial action. Previously, the valley was thought to have been formed solely by great earthquakes. His glacial theory, which was substantiated by measurements made of still-moving ice fields on the surrounding mountainsides, won Muir national and then world fame as a naturalist.

Muir had long been troubled by the westward advance of the logging industry. By the 1880s, man's ax and saw were beginning to attack vast stretches of far western lands and leaving behind stumps and crushed foliage where once there had been towering trees and the lush undergrowth and varied animal life that were found in their shade. Fearing that the forests surrounding his beloved Yosemite Valley would be the next victims, Muir began to write magazine articles warning of the damage being done to the country's wooded treasures and urging that Yosemite (which was a state park at the time) and two nearby regions of giant sequoias in the Sierra Nevada be set aside as national parks.

His campaign on behalf of the three areas met with success in 1890 when Congress established the Yosemite, Sequoia, and General Grant National parks. The General Grant Park, which was named for Ulysses S. Grant, the nation's eighteenth president, was allotted additional acreage in 1940, had its name changed, and became the Kings Canyon National Park of 461,901 acres. Today, the Sequoia Park covers some 402,482 acres; within its boundaries are groves of giant sequoias and 14,494-foot Mount Whitney, the highest peak in the United States outside Alaska. Yosemite, including its mountain regions and its 7-square-mile valley floor, occupies 761,170 acres.

Further accomplishments were achieved in later years. Muir and a number of friends founded the Sierra Club to enjoy the three parks and to keep a watchful eye on how they were being supervised and used. The club eventually became one of the largest and most influential conservation and environmental organizations in the world.

Then, in 1896, Muir met with President Grover Cleveland to voice his concern over the timber industry's increasingly savage cutting. By now, in the Midwest alone, logging axes and saws had pretty well stripped all the trees from an area the size of Europe. Mr. Cleveland shared the naturalist's concern and his desire to safeguard as much of the nation's forestland as possible. He asked Muir to head a national committee to prepare a report on what could be done to save the trees. When completed, the report advised that two new national parks be formed. As a result, the Mount Rainier National Park in the state of Washington and the Grand Canyon National Park in Arizona were formed. The first was established in 1899 and the second in 1919.

The Mount Rainier Park, lying on the forested slopes of an ancient volcano and spreading over the meadowlands at its base, covers 225,404 acres. The Grand Canyon Park was originally established as a forest reserve in 1893—three years before Muir met with President Cleveland. Later, part of it became a national monument and then, in 1919, a national park. Today, with the addition of lands in more recent years, it spreads over some 1.2 million acres.

In addition, the Muir report recommended that thirteen wooded areas in eight western states be set aside as national reserves, the name given to national forests prior to 1905.

Mr. Cleveland liked the idea of the reserves and authorized their establishment. As expected, the timber companies reacted angrily to his action. They quickly pressed their supporters in Congress to enact a bill canceling the authorization. Just as quickly, John Muir and his Sierra Club voiced their opposition to the proposed bill. He and the club members, plus their many supporters, besieged Congress with letters urging that it be defeated. In addition, the naturalist wrote numerous magazine articles in support of the reserves and won widespread public support for them. At first, it seemed as though his campaign had failed when the Senate passed the bill in 1898. But the House of Representatives, heeding the rising public support, defeated the measure and it was not passed into law.

Though spending much of his time writing nature books and magazine articles, Muir managed to travel often so that he could view nature in all its forms. A trip in 1879 took him to Alaska, where he won the distinction of being the first white man to visit the glacial region that eventually became the Glacier Bay National Park and Preserve of 3.2 million acres.

Then, in 1906, when he was sixty-eight years old, he hiked into the Arizona wilderness and came upon one of the state's petrified forests. Muir named his find the Blue Forest. It contains fossilized wood estimated to be 160 million years old, and is now a part of the Petrified Forest National Park. The park covers 93,532 acres and houses the world's largest display of wood that the ages have turned to brilliantly colored stone.

John Muir fell ill with pneumonia during a Christmas visit to his daughter's southern California home in 1914. He died there on Christmas Eve at age seventy-eight. Left behind was a lifetime of nature study, a series of books and magazine articles on the beauties and wonders found in the outdoors, and his greatest contribution of all—his work in furthering the growth of the National Park System.

Now we turn to the acts of Congress that, together with the efforts of John Muir and so many of his fellow preservation-minded Americans, contributed to the growth of the National Park System.

THE ANTIQUITIES ACT

As the twentieth century dawned, there was widespread concern over the harm that vandals, profiteers, and souvenir-hunting tourists were doing to Native American artifacts found in the Southwest. Vandals were defacing rock paintings and carvings. Profiteers and souvenir hunters were stealing pottery, carvings, and the remnants of bows and arrows. Hit especially hard were the archaeological diggings in the region.

Congress took action against the marauders by passing the Antiquities Act.[3] The measure, which was enacted in 1906, authorized the president to proclaim that areas especially rich in artifacts be set aside and safeguarded against future harm. As a result, twenty southwestern regions were placed under government protection within a decade. Many of them would later be designated as national parks. A quarter of all the facilities in the National Park System began as lands protected by the Antiquities Act.

THE NATIONAL PARK ACT

By 1916, the United States was able to boast thirteen national parks. They were all beauty spots, but they all shared two problems. The first was the need to improve their management; some were unsupervised while the supervision of others was left to the U.S. Army as an extra assignment. The second involved a dispute that centered on a government plan to develop an area within the Yosemite Park.

The U.S. Congress attempted to solve both problems by passing the National Park Act of 1916.[4] The act handled the first problem by calling for the creation of a new organization under the Department of the Interior, to be known as the National Park Service. The service would be responsible for the care and management of the National Park system's facilities.

The solution to the second problem lay in a key paragraph in the act, which stipulated that the lands in the system were to be managed and maintained in such a way "as will leave them unimpaired for the enjoyment of future generations."

The key word *unimpaired* was placed in the act because of a battle that preservationists had waged for years involving water interests over the Yosemite Park's Hetch Hetchy Valley. The battle had erupted when plans to build a dam across the valley were presented to the U.S. Congress for approval. The purpose of the dam, to be built with federal funds, was to flood the valley and turn it into a reservoir that would provide water for northern California farms and the city of San Francisco.

The plan had infuriated John Muir, who considered the Hetch Hetchy Valley almost as beautiful as the Yosemite Valley itself. With help from the Sierra Club and preservationists everywhere, Muir waged a campaign to have the plan discarded on the grounds that the dam would see a wondrous place flooded and lost to the people forever. But his voice went unheeded. In 1913, a year before the naturalist's death, Congress authorized the construction of the dam, which was built soon thereafter.

However, in 1916, members of Congress realized that the dam would indeed damage the beauty of Yosemite Park. In the National Park Act, they sought to correct matters and protect other Park System lands from similar fates by declaring that the lands were to be free of any commercial and industrial development that would sully the public's enjoyment of them.

Out of the work of John Muir and his fellow preservationists, and out of the Antiquities and National Park acts—and other laws—emerged the vast complex of public lands that make up today's National Park System. Vast as it is, the system today faces a number of threats.

3
OUR THREATENED NATIONAL PARKS

The principal threats to the beauty of the National Park System are two:

> An overload of tourists at certain times of the year.
>
> A number of human-caused problems not the fault of heavy tourism. Found both inside and outside the facilities, they are damaging the plant and animal life within the facilities.

THE TOURIST OVERLOAD

Each year millions of Americans spend their vacations seeking the outdoor recreation available in the National Park System. At present, the number of visitors to the system is the highest in history.[1] In 1989, the system absorbed upward of 265 million visitors, with 59 million of their number traveling to the national parks and preserves alone. Ten years earlier, in 1980, the visitors totaled 200 million. This indicates a 30 percent increase during the ten-year period between 1977 and 1987.

The Reasons for the Increase

Why this increase? Three reasons have been suggested. First, recent years have witnessed a growing appreciation of nature among countless Americans. The warnings of environmentalists that we are damaging—in some cases irreparably—our planet and its myriad life-forms with our smoke-belching industries; our logging, mining, and oil drilling activities; and our cars; have made more of us aware of the need to preserve the rich beauty of our natural wonders.

Second, vast numbers of Americans live in urban areas and endure on a daily basis the stresses of city life, such as air pollution, heavy traffic, jostling crowds, and the fast pace of life. More urban dwellers are turning to the outdoors to soothe their ragged spirits and find the peace and the beauty that can free them, at least for a time, from the pressures of their daily lives.

Finally, the U.S. population is growing older. The children born in the years following World War II are now middle-aged, and those who came along in the 1960s have reached their thirties. As younger people, they went in for strenuous recreational activities, such as tennis, biking, surfboarding, backpacking, and the like. Now, as they grow older, they are seeking quieter pursuits; this shift can be seen in the fact that the number of people backpacking into the wild and remote regions of the national parks decreased by half in the 1980s, while sojourns in the more comfortable central areas increased. Also, vacationing married couples and the parents of young children are interested in activities in which the entire family can participate; rather than settle for dirt trails, they want such accommodations as paved walkways along which baby carriages and strollers can easily travel. The opportunities for sight-seeing, camping, strolling, and nature study offered by many of the National Park System's facilities can fill the bill for them on both counts.

An Odd Battleground

The steady growth of tourism has put a heavy strain on the system's most popular facilities, and has turned them into an unusual battleground.[2] It is not a battleground on which environmentalists are struggling against commercial interests but a battleground for the visitors, one where the visitors often have to overcome the very problems they are attempting to escape—traffic gridlock and air pollution—before they can enjoy the park's facilities.

Consider the following examples:

> **Grand Canyon National Park.** *Annual visitors jumped from 2.5 million to 3.9 million in the years between 1986 and 1989. The increase has produced traffic gridlock at the canyon's popular South Rim, with the automobile exhaust contributing to a smog condition that obscures from view the canyon depths, its opposite rims, and its Colorado River. Joining the car-generated murk are two pollutants not of the visitors' making—first, haze from a coal-burning electric power plant located a hundred miles away; and, second, smog carried by the wind for some four hundred miles from Los Angeles.*
>
> **Wind Cave National Park.** *A South Dakota jewel, this facility of 28,292 acres features prairie wildlife and, below ground, a cave of 53 passages with unique calcite formations. The park attracted 1.25 million visitors in 1989 and was so crowded during peak times that waiting periods lasting an hour and a half to tour the cave were common.*
>
> **Yosemite National Park.** *Some 3.5 million people visited the park in 1989. The summer season*

alone drew 1.5 million of that number. They arrived in more than 500,000 cars, causing traffic to become so jammed that officials were forced to restrict entry to the park at times, a situation that disappointed and frustrated many of the vacationers. Each day, the visitors left behind twenty-five tons of trash and a million gallons of sewage.

Acadia (Maine), **Carlsbad Caverns** (New Mexico), **Crater Lake** (Oregon), **Grand Teton** (Wyoming), and **Voyageurs** (Minnesota) **National parks.** *All suffered severe overcrowding and its attendant traffic congestion at their peak times in 1989.*

Adding to the Strain

Another problem weighing on the system is a change recently noted in the American family's vacationing habits.[3]

There was a time when most Americans took annual vacations of two weeks to a month and spent a part of the time traveling. As shown by recent studies, this pattern began to change in the late 1980s. In 1985, the average length of U.S. vacations was 5.7 days, but by 1989 the average had dropped to 4.7 days. There seems to be two reasons for this. First, many families, eager to escape the stresses of their daily urban lives, have replaced the single yearly vacation with two or more vacations of shorter duration (often extended weekends) within the year.

Second, countless American families now form what are called two-income households, with both the husband and wife holding down jobs. A series of shorter vacations or extended weekends is seen as easier to arrange. They might find it difficult to have their employers give them both a longer vacation at the same time.

What the shorter vacation means is that, given the time to reach one of the system's facilities, the stay there is going to be brief—perhaps a night or two, perhaps just a few hours. The National Park Service estimates that an average visit to its facilities lasts a mere three and a half hours. So, the flow of traffic in and out of the facility, with the gridlock and frustration it triggers, is bound to be greater than ever before. A further result is that the vacationers do not give themselves the chance to visit the facility's various areas and truly enjoy the beauty there.

Possibly the briefest visits of all have been recorded at the Wupatki National Monument in Arizona. The monument, which is spread over 53,253 acres, features the ruins of red sandstone pueblos built by Native Americans nearly a thousand years ago. A team of researchers from Northern Arizona University spent seven weeks in 1989 studying the tourist habits at Wupatki. They found that 5 percent of the vacationers did not bother to visit the ruins but simply lingered long enough to buy postcards and mementos at the souvenir shop before departing. Only about 20 percent completed the walk along the one-third-mile path that led them around the monument's central ruin, a spectacular building of a hundred rooms interspersed with oval courtyards. According to the researchers, most vacationers were on their way out of the monument grounds after a mere twenty minutes.

Such brief stays have angered many other visitors. One Californian speaks for them all when he says, "You certainly get the impression that a lot of people are not really interested in seeing a park. All they want to do is be able to say that they've been there and get a few postcards and souvenirs to prove it. They're fouling up the air with their cars and getting in the way of all the rest of us who would like to enjoy the place."

The Californian's anger is shared by other people. Environmentalists and everyday people who love the outdoors are infuriated by the activities of some visitors to the facilities or to nearby spots. For instance, airboat rides on the waters outside the Everglades National Park in Florida are destroying fragile grasses, with the damage spreading to the grasses within the park. (Contributing also to the harm are the droughts that Florida has suffered in recent years.) Vandals have damaged ancient Native American carvings in the caves of Utah's Capitol Reef National Park. Officials there have also reported thefts of Native American artifacts from time to time. There have been some thefts of cactus plants at Big Bend National Park in Texas, and thefts of petrified wood at Arizona's Petrified Forest National Park.

Accommodations for the Visitors

The increasing number of visitors over the years has led to another problem for the system. Accommodations —among them, campgrounds, hotels, and cabins—must be built to serve their needs.[4] The system's facilities have always featured such accommodations, but the rise in tourism has required that additional ones be constructed. There is a growing feeling among environmentalists and others that these accommodations, especially the commercial concessions—the hotels, restaurants, and gift shops—are sullying the natural look of the facilities and running the risk of turning them into little more than citified theme parks.

A major case is the very popular Yosemite Park. For years, it has featured hotel, cabin, and campground accommodations. But they have grown steadily to meet the needs of the crowds that now flow into Yosemite annually. In sharp contrast to the national average of three hours and thirty minutes for a park visit, estimates hold that, of the 3.4 million visitors who arrived at Yosemite in 1989, upward of 95 percent spent one or more nights in a 4-square-mile area on the main valley floor. Located here are more than 1,000 buildings—hotels, cabins, restaurants, gift shops, and quarters for housing the park employees.

In the words of one Yosemite employee, the commercial concessions on the main valley floor are making the place look like a circus. Their number has resulted in a heated debate over the need and wherewithal to return the park to a more natural state. In chapter 4, we will describe a plan currently being proposed to achieve that goal.

State and Local Parks

The nation's state and local parks are suffering as much as the federal facilities from the visitor overload. In fact, they are likely to be suffering even more.[5] It is estimated that Americans spend 75 percent of their outdoor time in state and local parks. The remaining 25 percent is spent in Park System and privately owned facilities.

Karen L. Bowen, the president of the National Association of State Outdoor Recreational Liaison Officers (the organization that oversees the federal funds awarded annually to the states for their park systems), points up the state and local overload by using Minnesota's sixty-four state parks as an example. She says that in the three-year period between 1986 and 1989 the visits to the Minnesota parks jumped from 6 million to 10 million. Ten of the state's most popular parks suffer from continual congestion during peak times of the year.

NONTOURIST PROBLEMS

In the opinion of some system officials, overcrowding is far from being *the* major problem facing the National Park System. In all, the National Park Service has identified some 1,750 headaches besetting 200 of its most popular attractions. Ranking high among them are harms caused not by tourists but by other factors both inside and outside the facilities. We turn now to these nontourist factors.

Nontourist Damage: Inside the Facilities

Over the years, a number of plants and animals have been introduced into park areas and have ended up doing a considerable amount of harm to the native vegetation there.[6] Sometimes, the newcomers have been introduced to solve problems seen in or near the park areas, only to turn out to be a threat rather than a help. At other times, they have been accidentally introduced. Sometimes, they had been brought into an area for recreational purposes, often before the region ever became a parkland.

An example of a plant introduced to help solve a problem that has backfired can be found in the Great Smoky Mountains National Park, which occupies 529,269 acres in Tennessee and North Carolina and attracts over 10 million visitors annually. Some years ago, a vine called the oriental bittersweet was shipped in and planted to help control an eroding of the park soil caused by heavy rains and other factors. The vine has spread and is now strangling the facility's native trees.

Beginning more than a half-century ago, a variety of plants, among them the banana poka and the oriental ginger, was brought to the Hawaiian Islands to help prevent soil erosion and to add to the lushness of the already beautiful habitat. In the years since, they have spread over the land to such an extent that biologists now warn that they are choking out all the native Hawaiian plants. As a result, these native plants may soon completely disappear from such breathtaking spots as the 28,655-acre Haleakala National Park on the island of Maui.

A similar problem exists at the Grand Canyon National Park. The tamarisk tree was introduced there in the early 1920s to help retard soil erosion and to serve as a windbreak. Tamarisk trees now cover more than 200,000 acres, elbowing out the native trees and threatening the extinction of eight species of birds that nest among the native trees.

The Grand Canyon Park also suffers from the presence of a pest whose forebears were turned loose by early day western prospectors—the burro. The animal's descendants have grown into herds that are now happily devouring much of the park's vegetation. Several years ago, Grand Canyon officials launched a shooting program to reduce the size of the herds. The effort was halted because of a public outcry on behalf of the burros.

Now let's go back to Tennessee and North Carolina for a look at an animal that was set free to roam the Great Smoky Mountains Park long before it became a system facility. Brought to North Carolina in 1912 for recreational hunting purposes were wild boars. Many of them managed to escape the hunter's rifle and their descendants now abound throughout the park. One park official says that the boars, which can weigh up to four hundred and fifty pounds, will ravage anything that catches their attention.

Nontourist Damage: From the Outside

The National Park Service reports that of the 1,750 problems besetting its facilities, some 20 percent are not being generated within the facilities themselves. Rather, they are being created by urban and industrial developments outside the parks.

One of the most severe examples is the air pollution that pours in from both near and distant points. You'll recall that the murky smog staining the Grand Canyon is in part caused by a coal-burning electric plant a hundred miles away. The plant is the massive Navajo Generating Station, which was built in 1974 and ranks as one of the largest power operations in the country. Providing electricity to parts of Arizona, Nevada, and California, it burns 24,000 tons of coal per day. According to a 1987 study by the Park Service, its smoke emissions account for between 40 and 70 percent of the air pollution at the Grand Canyon during the winter months.

Other victims of airborne pollution include the Great Smoky Mountains Park and California's Sequoia and Kings Canyon National parks. Pollution is damaging the trees at all three locations and is said to be making them increasingly susceptible to various diseases. Still other pollution victims include Guadalupe Mountains National Park in Texas and the Shenandoah National Park in Virginia.

The trees of the Great Smoky Mountains and Guadalupe Mountains are also harmed by acid rain. Acid rain is rain that is shot through with a heavy concentration of sulfur. The sulfur reaches the parks in smoke borne by the winds from coal-burning factories and power stations, some of which lie hundreds—even thousands—of miles away.

Perhaps the saddest example the damage from surrounding urban and commercial development is evident in the Everglades National Park, which occupies part of America's largest and most prized wetland, the 10,000-square-mile Florida Everglades. The park is now called the country's most endangered national park because the Everglades are being used to provide water for nearby industrial and agricultural enterprises and for Florida's growing cities. This disruption of the region's water content is raising havoc with the wildlife in the park and throughout the Everglades. Adding to the tragedy is the fact that the waters are being tainted by chemicals and other discharges from farms and industries. A recent estimate by the National Audubon Society holds that the number of the wading birds in the Everglades, among them egrets and wood storks, has dwindled some 90 percent since the 1920s. The pesticides used in agriculture are accused of having reduced singlehandedly the population of nesting bald eagles by 70 percent.

We will talk more of the Florida Everglades and the park in chapter 5.

Despite the problems of overcrowding and the damage done by nontourist factors, a recent survey by the National Park Service showed that most visitors—some 80 percent or more[7]—enjoyed their stay once they were inside the facilities and out of their automobiles.

The findings may attest to the average American's patience and determination to enjoy a vacation no matter what the obstacles may be. But this doesn't mean that the National Park Service should do nothing about the system's many problems. Just what the Park Service—and the state parks—are doing to improve matters, plus what you can do to help, is the subject of our next chapter.

4
MEETING THE THREATS

What can be done to solve the many problems that plague our national and state parks? How can we:

Ease the overcrowding in many facilities?
Help people get more out of their visits in the short time they spend in the parks?
Prevent commercial accommodations and the regrettable behavior of some visitors from destroying the natural beauty of a park setting?
Reduce the damage done to the facilities by nontourist factors?

PROBLEM: OVERCROWDING

Steps are already being taken by both federal and state park officials to ease the burden of overcrowding.[1] Most states and a number of federal facilities currently require that vacationers make reservations for campsites and other lodgings in advance of their visits. One state, Nebraska, has undertaken a special program to avoid the overcrowding that has long troubled its highly popular North Platte River State Park. Every January, Nebraska holds a lottery, with the winners receiving the campground reservations for the year.

Whenever vacationers threaten the place with traffic gridlock, various federal and state parks restrict the number of cars permitted into a facility. When this happens, vacationers usually must park outside the grounds and enter the facility on foot or, if available, by shuttle.

At the state level, Minnesota is testing an approach that, if proven successful, might be worthwhile for other states to consider. With its most popular attractions facing constant overcrowding, Minnesota is publicizing its lesser-known parks in an effort to encourage vacationers to give them a try.

But the approach presents a problem for some potential visitors. The lesser-known parks often boast a more rugged terrain than the more popular spots and are not as accessible. Many families, especially those who take short vacations, are unwilling to travel the extra distance. Moreover, many would prefer the convenience of the family campgrounds, running water, and playground equipment usually found in the more popular parks rather than try the more rugged backpacking trails and spots for deep-woods camping offered by the lesser-known parks.

What You Can Do to Help

Every vacationer can do much to help ease the overcrowding problem by following a few simple rules. Here's how you as a vacationer can help when planning to visit a federal or state park:[2]

> **If possible, pick an off-season time for your visit, when the park is not as crowded as usual.** *For most facilities, the peak periods occur during the summer and over the weekends. July*

ranks as the most congested month of all. Estimates hold that some 121 million Americans depart for vacation during that month alone, with about 28 million of their number electing to enjoy some time in the outdoors.

On the other hand, some facilities, while crowded during the summer and at weekends, report that their peak periods come at other times of the year. For example, Virginia's Shenandoah National Park, with its marvelous forests, reports that its busiest month is October, when the trees sport their brilliant autumn colors.

So, unless your heart is set on seeing a certain park and you are free to visit it only during a peak period, schedule your vacation for a time when it will be less crowded. You may be disappointed to miss such natural extravaganzas as Shenandoah's fall colors, but your disappointment may be outweighed by the enjoyment of the facility when it's not caught up in a big-city traffic gridlock or buried under layers of your fellow tourists.

Try visiting a lesser-known park. *Why not put the Minnesota plan to personal use? When planning a vacation, check out those parks that are not especially well known. All the federal and state facilities are beauty spots, with some of the lesser-known ones being as or even more beautiful than their better-known counterparts. While some may not have all the comforts and accommodations you would like, they may still have enough to meet your needs. And, if you're looking for such hardy pleasures as backpacking and deep-woods camping, they will more than likely be exactly what you're looking for.*

Learn about the park you're planning to visit. *It's always wise—and, with the overcrowding,* *more and more necessary—to gather some basic information about a park before your visit. If you intend to stay overnight or for a few days, find out if the park offers overnight accommodations and if reservations are required for campsites or other types of lodging. If you're driving a recreational vehicle, such as a Winnebago, or pulling a trailer, make sure that the park can provide the water and electrical hookups you'll need. A number of parks are able to do so, but take no chances. Possibly the worst thing you can do is show up at a park without warning for a stay of one or more nights and discover there's no room for you. You've spoiled your vacation and have needlessly added a few more people to those already there.*

All the information you will need about a park, its accommodations, and the pleasures it has to offer is no farther away than your telephone. A phone call to the national or state park office in your area—or to the local office of your state automobile association—will either provide you with the needed information or tell you where it can be obtained. A directory and map of the entire National Park system can be obtained from the National Park Service.

PROBLEM: GETTING THE MOST OUT OF PARK VISITS

What can be done to lengthen the visits of so many vacationers (a national average of three and a half hours, you'll recall) and help the people to do something other than while away the time in a gift shop or restaurant while at a park? This question has elicited a number of recommendations from park officials and others.[3]

One suggestion comes from James S. Scull, a federal planner of outdoor recreation. He cites the fact that three-quarters of the American people live in urban areas. As a result, they tend to confine their short stay to the park's central grounds, and shy away from venturing farther afield because they are unacquainted with and consequently intimidated by the great outdoors. Scull believes it would be a good idea to establish what he calls "halfway outdoor areas," where urbanites are introduced to the outdoors at an easy pace before trying a larger park. They would then be better prepared to venture into areas and along trails outside the facility's central grounds.

Another suggestion comes from Dr. Robert Trotter, the professor of anthropology who headed the Northern Arizona University research team that studied the behavior of vacationers at Wupatki National Monument and found that the length of their visits to the site averaged out to twenty minutes. Dr. Trotter suggested that the monument's visitor center include a videotape presentation showcasing the Indian ruins that are Wupatki's centerpiece in an effort to encourage the vacationers to visit them. Though Dr. Trotter's suggestion is meant for the Wupatki Monument, it is one that could be adapted elsewhere.

Actually, a number of methods to stimulate visitor interest are already in use at many federal and state parks. It is not uncommon for visitor centers to feature videotapes, motion pictures, or photographic displays of a facility's popular attractions. Some facilities even feature "listening pads"—telephone-like devices that are installed at points of interest along trails and walkways. When you hold one to your ear, a recorded voice may describe the type of plant life you are seeing or the historical significance of the spot you are visiting.

Additionally, many federal and state facilities have long featured cultural events (for example, presentations on the historical or ecological significance of the facility) and guided activities (hikes, nature walks, visits to historic buildings). Unfortunately, however, a recent survey of federal park visitors showed that both cultural events and guided activities rank far down the list of features that attract people to the facilities.

The survey was conducted by the President's Commission on Americans Outdoors, which was formed by President Ronald Reagan in 1986. It listed the eleven features—or "attributes," as the commission called them—that Americans most want to see in a facility. Of the eleven, guided activities stood last on the list, while cultural events took seventh place.

Listed below, according to their importance in the eyes of visitors, are the eleven attributes most looked for in federal parks:

1. Natural beauty
2. How crowded the park is
3. Restroom facilities
4. Parking available
5. Available information
6. Picnic areas
7. Cultural events
8. Fees charged
9. Concessions (gift shops, restaurants, etc.)
10. Organized sports available
11. Guided activities

What You Can Do to Help

At first glance, there may not seem much—if anything—that you as an individual can do to change the visiting habits of the countless Americans who flock to our national and state parks. But this isn't quite true because there is a great deal you can do to change your own visiting habits and those of your family and friends. If each of us would concentrate on his or her own changes of habit, the effect would be nationwide. Here are some ideas that should be of help:

Don't let your fear of the outdoors spoil your visit. *If you're a city dweller, it is likely that you're intimidated by the outdoors. If so, your* *feelings are quite natural and to be expected. The wilderness is an unfamiliar place to you, and most humans are ill at ease when facing the unfamiliar. Further, certain parks do contain admitted dangers that you must watch out for. Some examples: There are a great many bears in Montana's Glacier National Park; a walk through the caves at New Mexico's Carlsbad Caverns National Park can be a slippery one; the buffalo at Wyoming's Grand Teton National Park are known to charge on occasion.*

But don't let the actual dangers in some parks, or your uneasiness spoil your enjoyment and keep you from seeing as much as possible of what a facility has to offer. To get the most out of your visit, you need not go charging along an unfamiliar trail. That can be downright foolish. Rather, take advantage of those last-place guided activities. You'll be under the supervision of a park ranger who knows the place, knows the dangers to avoid, and knows how to care for the people in his or her charge. If you prefer to go off by yourself, be sure to stick to designated trails.

Be prepared to enjoy yourself. *Even though you may feel a bit intimidated, arrive at the park with the idea of having a good time and seeing as much as you can see. In particular, don't make the mistake of thinking that a guided walk or hike is going to be too tiring or that a cultural event is going to be a bore. A good walk or hike, though tiring, can also be rewarding because you've seen some fascinating scenery. And don't turn your nose up at the term "cultural event." Give it a try. It's likely you'll be in for a surprise. Presentations on the history of the park, the customs and ways of life of the people who once lived there, and the animals that now inhabit it can be fascinating.*

As usual, learn something of the facility before your visit. *The one sure way to hinder your enjoyment is to arrive at a park and then wonder what there is to see and do. You'll either become discouraged and spend your visit hanging around the postcard display in the gift shop or lose some precious time finding out what the park has to offer and then deciding exactly what you'd like to see. Find out beforehand what you'd particularly like to do and see. Then, once you arrive at the park, you can add other attractions to your visit if time allows.*

PROBLEM: PRESERVING A PARK'S BEAUTY

Two points will be discussed here—first, the accommodations that are widely believed to be damaging the natural beauty of so many parks, and second, the acts of vandalism and theft that invariably mar the beauty of their victims.[4]

Accommodations

In the minds of some people, the addition of even one commercial accommodation—one souvenir shop or restaurant—reduces the natural beauty of a park. Actually, the problem of developing commercial accommodations that finally begin to threaten the surrounding beauty is one that chiefly bothers those parks whose cabins, hotels, shops, and such are constructed in places where they block the view of major beauty spots, as well as parks with central grounds within a confined area.

Two cases in point here are California's Sequoia and Yosemite parks. Sequoia suffers from the first problem. The second problem has long been a headache for Yosemite, with its central grounds located on a valley floor surrounded by towering peaks. Each park is currently planning to correct matters.

The Plans for Sequoia

The Sequoia park, which welcomes about a million visitors a year, celebrated its hundredth anniversary (as did Yosemite) in 1990. It spent its centennial year planning to move the park's accommodations and commercial concessions out of what is known as the Giant Forest because they have long blocked and sullied the view of sequoia trees, which are the largest living things on earth. Scheduled to be moved are cabins, a lodge, a motel, and a collection of barrackslike buildings that house employees. One especially bothersome building due for removal is not a commercial structure but a projection shack for the slide pictures of the park that are shown to visitors at nightly campfires. The shack sits at the base of one of the finest trees in the Giant Forest.

The buildings slated for removal will be replaced by a visitor center located several miles away. The center will feature a lodge for overnight guests and various concessions for all visitors. The removal of the present buildings and the construction of the new visitor center are scheduled to be completed by 1993.

The Plans for Yosemite

All the accommodations and commercial concessions at Yosemite—a total, you'll recall, of more than a thousand buildings consisting of hotels, campgrounds, restaurants, cabins, gift shops, and lodgings for the park employees—are contained within a four-square-mile area of the valley floor. The remainder of the park, some 97 percent of its area, lies outside the valley and remains uncluttered and beautiful to see.

Yosemite officials have long been worried that the maze of buildings has damaged the valley's natural beauty. In 1980, they developed a plan to restore the valley to a more natural state by cutting back on both the heavy traffic flow and the number of accommodations. The plan called for the elimination of a thousand parking spaces and a ban on auto entry, with visitor cars to be replaced by shuttle buses that would run from outside the valley or beyond the park boundaries. As for the buildings, many would be removed and placed elsewhere. Slated for removal were offices, housing for some of the employees, and nonessential shops and stores. Overnight accommodations were to be cut by 268 units.

There was little action on the plan throughout the decade, in great part because of budgetary problems. In 1982, 600 parking spaces were eliminated. There were some shuttle buses in use at the time of the plan's formulation and a few were added to their number. Several buildings were removed, chief among them a sewer plant and the residences of some rangers. The proposed cut of 268 overnight accommodations came to nothing. Rather, 21 overnight units were added by the Curry Company, the firm that provided all the park's commercial services—hotels, cabins, stores, restaurants, and others. The new overnight units were placed within existing buildings.

At present, however, the park officials are studying the plan anew, with an eye to strengthening or revising it for future use. Their work has triggered a variety of contrasting reactions from fans of Yosemite. Some people are not bothered by the buildings, feeling that once a visitor leaves the structures behind, Yosemite immediately greets the eye with one scenic wonder after another. Others hate the buildings and want to see as many as possible removed. Still others like the comfort and convenience provided by the accommodations and voice no objection to others being added if needed.

In the study, the Yosemite officials are facing several decisions. Should they allow the park accommodations to increase to meet the mounting flood of visitors? Should they halt all future commercial development and remove the buildings already erected and in use? Should they forbid all vehicular entry, insisting that tourists leave their cars elsewhere and then enter by means of a shuttle system? The answers to these questions should be heard sometime in the early 1990s.

From the start of the study, two organizations that would be made deeply interested in the approaching decisions were—the Curry Company and the Yosemite Restoration Trust. The Curry Company has handled all of Yosemite's commercial concessions since 1925 and opposed the study. Curry feared that radical changes in the park's operation would result in a heavy loss of revenue. Further, should the park officials decide on a heavy reduction in accommodations, the company also feared that they might not renew its contract with Yosemite. The current contract expires in 1993.

The Yosemite Restoration Trust is a nonprofit organization of well-known California nature lovers. It was formed soon after the study began. Its aim is to win out over the Curry Company in 1993 and be awarded the new contract for running the park's commercial operations. If successful, the trust wants to reduce the number of commercial concessions and funnel much of the earnings of those remaining into the maintenance of the park.

On being formed, the trust pointed out that the annual budget for the operation of Yosemite has remained much the same for the past ten years while park attendance has multiplied 30 percent. Along with many environmentalists, the members of the trust were angry with the Curry Company on two counts. First, they contended that it cares little for keeping Yosemite in its natural state but is principally interested in reaping greater profits by developing further commercial facilities. Second, Curry pays the federal government a fee of three-fourths of 1 percent on its gross annual sales. In 1988, gross sales amounted to $76.1 million, out of which the government received $570,774. The trust members said that was a mere pittance, especially in a time when the annual budgets assigned to national park facilities are lower than the costs of operating them.

The Curry Company responded that its concessions are enjoyed and required by many of the park visitors and that, in adding new concessions over the years (recently, a new pizza parlor and ice-cream stand were opened), it was keeping pace with the needs of the increasing flow of tourists.

In 1991, the Curry Company came under Japanese ownership. The Music Corporation of America (MCA) entertainment conglomerate, of which Curry is a part, was bought by Matsushita Electric Industrial Company. The Yosemite situation changed soon after. Matsushita announced that it did not wish to continue running the park's concessions. Curry would no longer seek the concession contract.

In September 1991, Matsushita turned over its concession rights to a nonprofit organization, the National Park Foundation. The Foundation will now accept bids on a concession contract to be awarded in 1993. The Yosemite Restoration Trust plans to continue its efforts to win the contract.

Vandalism and Theft

All parks, federal and state alike, are aware that vandalism and theft are constant dangers and are on the alert for them. Park personnel have the power to apprehend vandals, thieves, and other troublemakers. Some very large facilities even have their own jails and courthouses. But vandals and thieves present a problem so far as apprehension is concerned. They are sneaks who operate quickly and when no one is looking. Further, many thieves are otherwise honest citizens momentarily overcome by the desire to take away a "souvenir," making it difficult for a park official to treat them with the severity that many people think they deserve.

In the simplest of ways, you can be of great help in the control of both vandalism and theft. Make sure that you, your family, and your friends are never responsible for even the slightest act of vandalism—not the scratching of your initials into a tree, nor the theft of something as little as a rock. Again, as in the case of changing visiting habits, if each of us would take care never to be a vandal or a thief, the effect would be nationwide.

In matters of theft and vandalism, always follow this old bit of national park advice: Take nothing but photographs. Leave nothing but footprints.

And let us add one point. Even more harmful than vandalism and theft to a park's beauty are littering and fire. Instances of vandalism and theft are actually few compared to the amount of littering that every facility sees daily. Look for a trash bin for your empty soda container. Or carry a small bag in which your litter can be stored for later disposal in a bin.

Littering, incidentally, can also be a danger for you and your fellow visitors. There are cases where such animals as bears have come foraging for discarded food and then have attacked passersby.

As for fire, is it necessary to remind anyone of good sense to be very careful when building and extinguishing campfires? Or to warn against throwing away used matches without first making absolutely certain that they are out and have cooled to the point where they are no longer dangerous? Or to say that the tossing aside of a cigarette is the action of a fool?

PROBLEM: NONTOURIST DAMAGE

Chapter 3, as you'll recall, first dealt with a nontourist problem that has occurred inside many facilities—the sometimes deliberate and sometimes unintentional introduction of plants and animals that have gone on to harm the plants and animals native to the site.

The job of undoing the harm that has been done—the uprooting of thousands of acres of injurious plants, for example—promises to be both physically and economically impossible. And so the aim should be to avoid future harm. Toward this end, The Wildlife Society, an international environmental group, offers the following approach to control future damage by what it calls "exotic species," a term that encompasses both the plants and animals alien to an area.[5] The society holds that exotic flora and fauna should be introduced into an area only after competent scientists have demonstrated that:

> *(a) the exotic can potentially satisfy a specific recreational or biological need in the ecosystem to which it will be introduced, (b) the exotic is ecologically suitable for introduction into the new ecosystem, (c) the exotic will not be deleterious to desirable species (native or exotics) or cause any deterioration of the ecological complex . . .*

Further, to protect against plants that, after being installed beyond an area's boundaries, will eventually work their way inside its confines, the society urges that:

> *No state, provincial, or national agency shall introduce, or permit to be introduced, any exotic species into any area within its jurisdiction unless such species can be contained exclusively within that jurisdiction, or unless adjoining jurisdictions into which the species could spread have sanctioned the introduction officially.*

The Wildlife Society, founded in 1937, is a nonprofit organization with more than 8,700 members in more than forty countries.

The society's approach is widely considered a sensible one. But what of the suffering that many federal, state, and local parks, from the largest to the smallest, are enduring from the nontourist damages—the air pollution and acid rain—that are borne to them on the winds from far outside their boundaries? The unfortunate answer is that at present, they are powerless to defend against them. Air pollution and acid rain are just two of the many evils that have led to the appearance of a worldwide problem—the poisoning of our planet's atmosphere through the increasing release into the air of industrial smoke, chemicals, gases, and automobile fumes. We can only hope that the nations of the world will find solutions to the serious problem of air pollution, before our atmosphere and all the earth's localities—from the largest cities to the smallest parks—and all of its life systems are harmed beyond repair. It is an effort that every one of us not only should but must support.

We turn now to the damage being done to one of America's premier national parks—the Everglades National Park—by the agricultural and industrial activities outside its borders. The park occupies a portion of the Florida Everglades, the largest wetland region in the United States. The sad fate befalling the park and the entire Everglades area is covered in the next chapter because it opens the way to discussing the fate of all the nation's watery tracts, not only our wetlands but our lakes, rivers, and coastlines as well.

5
OF WETLANDS, LAKES, RIVERS, AND COASTS

America's watery tracts—its wetlands, rivers, lakes, and coastlines—were once magnificent parts of the nation's wilderness. Today, many are still located in wilderness regions while others are now highly urbanized and industrialized. But they all have one problem in common. As is the Everglades National Park, their existence is threatened by pollution and a complex of industrial, agricultural, and recreational activities. Beginning with the Everglades tragedy, we'll look at representative examples of the harm that is occurring all across the nation.

THE EVERGLADES IN DANGER

Established in 1947, the Everglades National Park covers almost 1.4 million acres (some 2,200 square miles).[1] It lies along the southwestern coast of Florida and takes up about one-fifth of the Everglades area. The entire Everglades area encompasses some 10,000 square miles rich in swamps, mangrove forests, and myriad varieties of plant, fish, and animal life. The Everglades is actually a fifty-mile-wide river of slow-moving fresh water. The park lies at its mouth.

The Everglades—and, consequently, the park—are beset by several dangers. One is the loss of water that has been drained away to supply Florida's cities (especially Miami) during the state's recent years of urban growth and severe droughts. Another is pollution.

It is decades of pollution—the result of surrounding agricultural and industrial work—that is a chief threat to the plant and animal life in the Everglades and the park. As you'll recall from chapter 3, it has diminished the number of wading birds there, among them egrets and wood storks, by a staggering 90 percent since the 1920s. Agricultural pesticides are being blamed for having reduced the population of nesting bald eagles by a tragic 70 percent.

The Steps Leading to Danger

The problems that have haunted the Everglades can be traced to 1948 when the federal government, in an effort to broaden and stimulate Florida's economy, had the Army Corps of Engineers build 1,400 miles of canals and dikes just below Lake Okeechobee. The lake lies immediately to the north of the Everglades and is the chief source of Florida's water. The purpose of the canals and dikes was to drain 700,000 Everglade acres so that they could be used for agriculture. On being drained, they were given over mostly to sugarcane farming.

The system of canals and dikes enabled water engineers to control the amount of water entering or leaving Lake Okeechobee and the Everglades. Trouble first loomed for the Everglades in the early 1970s, when Florida was struck by a series of severe droughts. The engineers decided to use the canal/dike system to raise the water level in the Everglades during the annual dry season. Although well-intentioned, the move turned out to be a frightening mistake. The engineers did not realize that the Everglades' plants and animals were accustomed to and depended on definite dry and wet seasons for their survival. The raising of the Everglades water by just a few inches during the dry seasons disrupted the life cycle of these plants and animals and began to put their well-being in jeopardy.

Later in the 1970s, another danger became evident. Lake Okeechobee underwent a drastic change. Toxic algae and other plants suddenly appeared and began to threaten the lake's native plants and fish by devouring the oxygen content in its waters. The problem was blamed on the runoff from nearby dairy farms and from the 700,000 acres that had been converted to sugarcane farmland. The runoff was rich in phosphorus, a nutrient that was triggering the growth of the new plant life and algae. The phosphorus was contained in manure flowing in from the dairy farms. It was also being released from the converted acres as their soil decayed.

At that time, the runoff from the converted acres was being pumped into Okeechobee via the canal/dike system. Now an attempt was made to alleviate the lake's problems by reversing the process and pumping the lake's waters into the Everglades. According to environmentalists, the result proved to be an ecological disaster. The phosphorus-rich lake water triggered a burst of new plant life in the Everglades waterways. Since then, by voraciously eating up the oxygen content, the newcomers have been choking out the native plants and sickening and driving off the animals in the waterways. Among the most damaging of the newcomers is the cattail. At present, it is said to be spreading through the Everglades at a rate of four acres a day.

Worsening matters for the Everglades are the various pollutants—chemicals, herbicides, and pesticides—that flow in from surrounding agricultural and industrial operations. For example, in late 1989, the fish in most areas of the Everglades were declared unsafe to eat because they contained high levels of mercury. The presence of mercury has also resulted in a ban on the hunting of alligators. Their meat has been found to be dangerously contaminated with the chemical.

These problems, of course, tragically affect the health of waters, plants, and animals in the Everglades National Park. Federal and state officials alike are attempting to solve these problems, and a number of possible solutions are presently being considered.

Possible Solutions

For one, some water officials would like to see the Florida government take over a 40,000-acre strip of state and privately owned Everglades land. The acreage, which lies between Lake Okeechobee and the main area of the Everglades, would then be used as a temporary storage site for water being pumped from the lake. The water would remain at the site for eight days before being released into the Everglades. In that time, the plants there would absorb most of the water's phosphorus content and make it safe for its movement onward.

The plan is vehemently opposed by environmentalists. They contend that it deliberately sentences the animals and plants that thrive in those 40,000 acres to death.

Another plan calls for Congress to add 100,000 acres to the Everglades National Park to ensure that they will be safe from future agricultural work.

While these and other plans are being discussed and debated, environmentalists warn that something must be done. The harm being inflicted on the entire area is reaching into the Everglades National Park, causing it to be called the most endangered national park in the United States. Its beauty and its wildlife might well be destroyed in just a few more years.

OTHER WETLAND DAMAGE

But what of the country's other wetland regions? Are they, too, being harmed by pollution from inside and outside their boundaries? For the answer, we need only look to two federal refuges for waterfowl in the Far West.

In the 1980s, both the marshy, 5,900-acre Kesterson National Wildlife Refuge in California and the Stillwater National Wildlife Refuge in Nevada were seriously threatened by high levels of toxins in the waste water that flowed into them from surrounding agricultural operations.[2] Scores of dead birds were found at both facilities, and thousands of dead fish at Stillwater. Many of the animals at Kesterson were sick or deformed, as were chicks that were born without legs and eyes.

A 1986 survey by the Fish and Wildlife Service of the Department of the Interior revealed that eighty-five animal refuges across the nation were suffering from proven, suspected, or potential harms from the agricultural waste water entering their territories.

Along with damage being done, the country has also lost vast tracts of public and privately owned wetlands to agricultural and industrial developments and to such recreational developments as summer homes and resorts. In all, these developments and the pollution generated by them have contributed greatly to harming and destroying more than half of the nation's 215 million acres of U.S. wetlands since the 1950s.

Among the losses over the years have been 20 million acres of forested wetlands, swamps, rivers, and lakes along the lower Mississippi River. They were drained to make way for soybean farming and other agricultural work. Fortunately, a new effort is under way to restore some of the agricultural land—land considered of marginal value for farming—to its original wetland state rather than allowing it to lie fallow. For a start, 20,000 acres near Vicksburg, Mississippi, are being allowed to revert to their original forest cover.

The federal government has begun to realize that the nation has suffered too great a loss of its wetlands. In 1989, the government adopted a policy of what is called "no net loss" for federally owned wetlands. The policy, with certain exceptions, requires that any developer who fills in a wetland in one area must create or restore a wetland of equal size in another area.

LAKES IN DANGER

Thousands of lakes of varying size throughout the eastern United States are said to be suffering environmental harm from the phenomenon known as acid rain.[3] The story of acid rain dates back to the 1970s when the press began reporting that an odd rainfall was striking not only the eastern United States but also southeastern Canada. It contained a high degree of acidity that, according to the reports, was poisoning and killing plant and animal life in no fewer than 50,000 lakes in the two areas.

At that time, the term "acid rain" was a strange and frightening one for Americans everywhere. It is, however, no longer a stranger. In the years since, we have learned that acid rain is rain laced with a high acidic content. The acid is contained principally in the sulfur dioxide that pours skyward in smoke when coal and other fossil fuels are burned. Considered chiefly responsible for the acid rain in the eastern United States and southeastern Canada are the coal-burning industrial and electric power plants that dot the American Midwest. Also sharing the blame are a number of Canadian factories and smelting plants.

The midwestern coal-burning plants are able to harm the regions to their east because the prevailing winds in the United States come from the west. The winds capture the sulfur-laden smoke as it rises from the plant smokestacks and transport it eastward. As it travels, it spreads out over an area that extends from the New England states (except Maine) in the North to such southern states as Kentucky, Virginia, and the Carolinas. In route, it passes over Ohio, Pennsylvania, and New York.

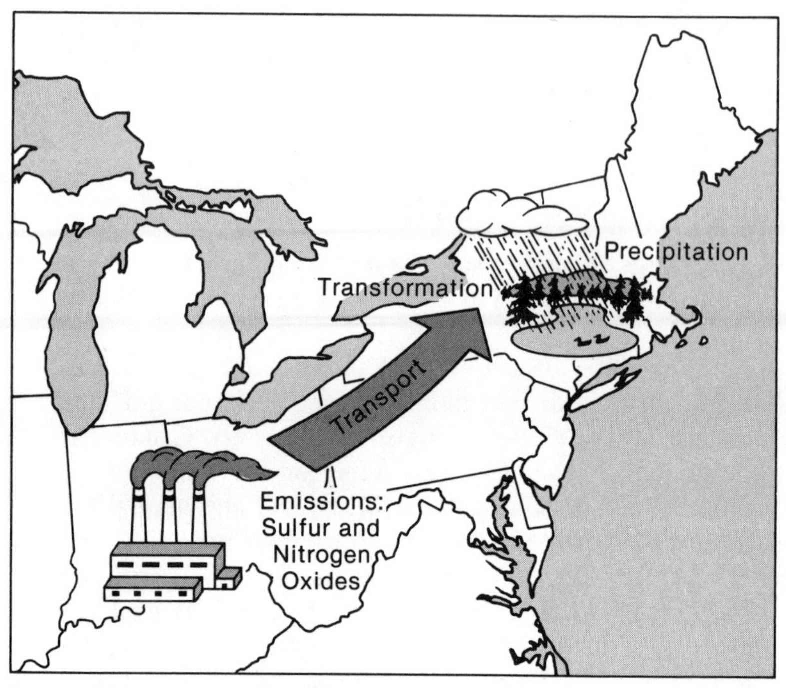

Figure 3. How Acid Rain Is Formed

John Muir (right), resting here
with fellow naturalist John Burroughs,
successfully campaigned to have
forest lands set aside
as national parks.

Loggers followed the nineteenth-century settlers westward, leveling acres of forest—as seen in these Minnesota woods—to clear land and provide lumber for homes.

Above: Environmentalists want to ensure that commercial developments, shown at their worst in this strip lining a road to the Grand Canyon, are kept from encroaching on the serenity of the parks, as seen, left, at Vernal Falls in Yosemite National Park.

Air pollution, crowds, noise, and all the stresses of urban life lead increasing numbers of Americans to retreat to the peace and beauty of the National Park System.

Overuse, littering, vandalism,
and lack of concern—as seen in
these dune-buggy tracks marring
the beauty of the desert floor—are
among the human-caused problems
besetting our parks and wildernesses.

By choosing lesser-known parks, and visiting during off-peak periods, vacationers lessen impact on an area and avoid the crowds that can spoil a wilderness experience.

When trees such as these in a Montana forest are cut down for lumber, many species of plant and animal life are also lost.

As pollution spreads into the air and waters of our national parks, above, bald eagles and other animal life disappear; dead fish, left, provide silent evidence of the contamination.

Left: Foreign plants and animals introduced into park areas have caused damage. The oriental ginger, originally brought to the Hawaiian Islands to prevent soil erosion, is choking native plants. Burros turned loose, below, by early prospectors have multiplied and are destroying vegetation in the Grand Canyon.

In clear-cut logging, a tract of land is stripped of all trees. Vegetation and undergrowth then are burned.

Nineteenth-century naturalist John Marsh warned of the soil erosion, floods, and mudslides that follow unrestricted use of the ax.

Conservationist Gifford Pinchot,
as the first chief of the Forest Service,
persuaded President Theodore Roosevelt
to place millions of acres in the forest
reserve program.

An Earth First! group protests
Forest Service proposals that
would allow clear-cutting,
and the use of roadways and
off-road vehicles in national forests.

The Northern Spotted Owl, a resident of old-growth forests, was at the center of the battle between environmentalists and the Pacific Coast logging industry.

At a "Save America's Forests" rally in Washington, D.C., participants voiced their distress over logging in the forest lands.

To environmentalists, old-growth forests are national treasures.

On mingling with the clouds during the trip, the sulfur falls with the rain—the acid rain—that visits these regions.

A Heated Debate

With the press continuing to report its many hazards, acid rain remains a frightening phenomenon for today's public. But, within the scientific world, how much injury it *actually* causes is the subject of heated debate. Some scientists contend it is wreaking terrible havoc on the lakes. In the opposite camp are scientists who doubt that it is solely or even chiefly responsible for the villainies attributed to it. They argue that other factors may also be at fault.

Each side has presented evidence to support its views. For example, the scientists who fear that acid rain is responsible for much harm point to a recent experiment conducted by Canadian researchers. The researchers deliberately increased the acid content in a lake that had hardly been touched by the rain. Results from the experiment seemed to indicate that the increased acid content stopped the lake's fish from reproducing and killed the crustaceans living on its bottom.

The opposing camp, however, points to a team of scientists that studied some 2,800 lakes devoid of fish in the Adirondacks, a mountain chain in New York State hard hit by acid rain in recent years. In 1988, the team members issued a report stating they could blame acid rain for the absence of fish in only 10 percent of the lakes.

They announced that other factors could be just as much to blame as acid rain for the "fishless lakes." Those factors included the acidity in the soils around the lakes, the acidic content in fertilizers entering the lakes from nearby farming operations, the types of vegetation growing on the lake bottoms, and the chemical content of the water in individual lakes. They pointed out that some of the lakes have always had such a high acid content that they were devoid of fish before there was ever such a thing as acid rain.

Consequently, the team members felt that acid rain could not be *solely* blamed for the absence of fish in the lakes. It could not be blamed at all in some instances. In others, it could be blamed for much damage and in still others for only a slight damage. In all, they felt that acid rain joins a number of other natural factors in increasing the acidity in a lake or in accelerating the formation of the acidity. This view of acid rain is shared by most scientists today.

The research team is part of a scientific task force, known as the National Acid Precipitation Assessment Program, organized by Congress in 1980 to study the acid rain problem and make recommendations for solving it. Its membership is made up of representatives from four national research laboratories, twelve government agencies, and upward of four hundred scientists from the United States and Canada. The research team's 1988 findings were contained in an interim report of the task force's work. The final report, with recommendations for handling the acid rain problem, is expected sometime in the early 1990s.

The interim report immediately triggered objections from a number of environmentalists, among them several government scientists. They criticized the report because it concerned only the findings in larger lakes and, as a consequence, had given an incomplete picture of what was happening in the Adirondacks. They contended that it should have also included findings in smaller lakes—especially those under ten acres in size. There, the effects of the acid rain were obviously being more severely felt and, thus, could be more clearly seen. The environmentalists claimed that from 10 to 19 percent of the smaller Adirondack lakes are the victims of highly dangerous acid levels.

Acid rain also stands accused of causing severe damage to forests. The research team members studied the

Adirondack forests and reported that much of the harm they had seen, such as defoliation and stunted growth, might not have been of acid rain's making alone. Some of the harm might have been caused by smog, fires, insect attacks, chemical changes in the surrounding soil, and droughts that have plagued parts of the world in recent years. This was contrary to environmental findings of the trees in two widely separated areas—the forests on Mount Mitchell in North Carolina and those in the western regions of Germany.

Mount Mitchell has long suffered from extremely polluted air, registering an acid content similar to that found in vinegar. Studies conducted at sixteen locations on the mountain have shown that its trees are experiencing quickening rates of defoliation and death, with the death rate ascending from around 10 percent in 1984 to approximately 40 percent just three years later. In western Germany, the forests endure a heavy onslaught of acid rain because of nearby industrial activity. The trees there have shown a slower-than-usual growth rate in recent years. Environmentalists have blamed the trouble in both areas on acid rain.

Fighting Acid Rain

Though scientists disagree on how serious the acid rain problem actually is, the United States is treating it as a very real environmental menace. It is the only safe course to take until all the facts about acid rain are gathered. Industry, the states, and the federal government have taken a number of actions against it. For one, a number of industrial and electric power plants, on their own or on orders from the states, have installed scrubbers in their smokestacks. Scrubbers are devices that cleanse the sulfur from smoke passing up the stacks. Some plants are looking at other sulfur-cleansing methods, among them a system that removes the substance from coal prior to burning.

These measures, however, have been employed by

only a few of the plants. Their use is widely opposed by the manufacturing and electrical power industries. Industry representatives say that the installation of such equipment as scrubbers is expensive. The costs would hurt the American consumer, who would be forced to pay higher prices for manufactured goods and electric power.

It has also been suggested that the plants turn to the use of coal with a low sulfur content. Again, there are objections from the manufacturing and power industries, because most of the coal deposits near the midwestern plants yield soft coal, which is heavily laced with sulfur. Hard coal with its lower sulfur content is to be found at a greater distance from the plants and would entail the expense of transporting it to its final destination for burning. That expense would have to be passed on to American consumers.

At the federal level, Congress has been wrestling with the overall problem of pollution ever since the 1950s, when it passed a measure that provided the states with funds to help them ease their individual dangers. In 1963, Congress enacted the Clean Air Act, which upped the amount of funds to go to the states. The additional funds failed to stem a menace that was growing yearly. The act was thus amended in 1970, with Congress setting standards meant to lower the amounts of the worst pollutants in our air, among them lead, carbon monoxide, and the hydrocarbons. Even though acid rain had not yet made itself felt, sulfur was high on the list of toxins to be attacked. It was coming not only from smokestacks but also from the exhaust systems of the nation's cars.

The amended act led to the reduction of some atmospheric pollutants but did not achieve as much as the government desired. Consequently, in 1989 President George Bush called for a new Clean Air Act with even more stringent air standards for the nation. Over the next months, a committee made up of members from the Senate and House of Representatives worked out the details of the proposed bill. The measure then went before Congress and won passage in late October 1990, after which it was signed into law by Mr. Bush.

The new Clean Air Act calls for massive cuts in the emissions of the nation's chief atmospheric contaminants. In the matter of acid rain, it requires the United States to cut its sulfur emissions by 10 million tons a year by the turn of the century. Also due to be cut in half are emissions of nitrogen oxide, a chemical that joins sulfur in creating acid rain.

The reductions are to be achieved by requiring the 111 largest coal-burning electric power plants in twenty-two states to meet strict new air standards through such measures as adopting new sulfur-cleansing technologies for their smokestacks or switching to the use of coal with a lower sulfur content.

RIVERS IN DANGER

For untold centuries, salmon have returned each year from the Pacific Ocean and have traveled up Washington and Oregon's Columbia River and on to the Snake River in Idaho to spawn. But over the years the increasing use of the waters in the two rivers for agricultural and industrial purposes has caused an alarming drop in the number of returning salmon. Largely responsible for the decline are the twelve dams that have been built along the Columbia, the Snake, and their tributaries to provide the surrounding industries, farmlands, and homes with hydroelectric power. They block—or, at the least, make difficult—the passage of the fish.[4]

It has been estimated that between 10 and 20 million salmon made the annual spawning run in the late 1800s. Their number has steadily plunged until it stands at 2.5 million today. Of that total, a mere 20 percent arrive from the Pacific. The rest are fish raised in the hatcheries that have been built along the rivers to offset the ever-dwindling number of returnees.

So alarming has the decline been that three salmon species—the sockeye, chinook, and coho—are now being considered for placement on the nation's Endangered Species List. This list is maintained by the U.S. Fish and Wildlife Service (FWS) of the Department of the Interior. It came into being when the U.S. Congress, worried over the number of animals being rendered extinct by industry, agriculture, and commercial recreation, passed the Endangered Species Act in 1973. The act made it a criminal offense for a commercial operation, government agency, or individual to threaten the survival of any animal species that has been placed on the Endangered Species List. Steps must be taken to protect that animal and its home. At present, the list contains the names of more than five hundred animals.

If the salmon are placed on the list, the stinging consequences will be felt by everyone in the Columbia and Snake area. The listing could mean that less river water will be allowed to flow to the surrounding farmlands for irrigation. Less hydroelectric power will be available from those twelve dams, a decrease that will cause industries, farming operations, and ordinary households to pay higher electric bills while receiving less electricity. It could reduce the amount of commercial and recreational fishing in the region. Long ago, the Indian tribes in Oregon and Washington were granted certain salmon fishing rights on the rivers, rights that could now be placed in jeopardy. The reduction in commercial salmon fishing could also extend into the Pacific and have an adverse effect on the livelihoods of fishermen and fishery workers clear up to Alaska.

Oregon, Washington, and their industries, long aware of declining salmon returnees, have spent hundreds of millions of dollars on facilities intended to help the fish on their trip to and from the spawning grounds. For example, ladders and screens have been constructed to help the fish get past the river dams. In addition, hatcheries have been built to increase the salmon population.

As ambitious as these projects have been, they have not been able to halt the steady decline in the number of salmon arriving to spawn. At present, the question of whether to place the sockeye, chinook, and coho salmon on the Endangered Species List is being studied by the National Marine Fisheries Service. The service is expected to announce its decision sometime in the early 1990s.

Polluted Waterways

In 1989, the Environmental Protection Agency (EPA), the federal office charged with assessing and controlling the nation's environmental problems, announced that at least 17,365 American rivers, streams, and bays suffer pollution from the industries, cities, towns, and military bases alongside or near them. Data in these waterway reports were filed with the agency by all fifty states and the five U.S. territories.

The 17,365 waterways represent approximately 10 percent of all American waters. They are reported as being laden with both natural and human-caused pollutants. The human-caused contaminants—which are mainly discharged from factories, sewage disposal plants, and storm drainage systems—include the metals cadmium and lead, pesticides, herbicides, and solvents. The natural pollutants are principally algae and bacteria.

States with more than 1,000 polluted waterways include West Virginia (1,745), Minnesota (1,140), Wisconsin (1,124), and Illinois (1,069). Reported among the states as having more than 500 such waterways are Kansas (922), New York (758), and Mississippi (529). Those states with under 100 include Indiana (35), Kentucky (26), and Georgia (23).

Reported by the states was pollution in excess of the amounts set in their standards for safe water. The EPA said that the state standards that measure pollution are designed to protect waterfowl and that the levels of pollution mentioned in the reports do not necessarily suggest a threat to human health. At the same time, however, the EPA said that the pollutants reported by the states did not cover all known cancer-causing chemicals and that the actual extent of pollution in the waterways may be far greater than indicated.

The EPA stated that the polluters are under orders to reduce the pollution and bring the waterways up to the standards set by the federal government for clean water by 1992.

The Troubled Mississippi

Among the most polluted of the nation's rivers is also one of its most majestic—the 2,500-mile-long Mississippi that flows from deep in Minnesota in the north to the Gulf of Mexico in the south. In 1988, Greenpeace USA, the American branch of the international environmental organization, made a comprehensive study of the Mississippi and reported that the industries, cities, and towns all along its length are poisoning it with toxic wastes. Greenpeace USA charged that "billions of pounds" of hazardous chemicals and heavy metals were pouring into the river every year.

Newsweek magazine writer Jerry Adler, in a 1990 article on the health of the Mississippi, wrote that Greenpeace was making the situation look especially deplorable by including such nontoxins as iron among the heavy metals. Still, he left no doubt that the river's health is bad enough even without the inclusion of the nontoxins.

The various discharges flow in from the surrounding states. They come from factories, farmlands, sewage disposal operations, drainage systems, and the commercial and pleasure boats that ply the river's waters. In some areas, people fear that the water is not safe to drink and that the fish are unfit to eat. Sixty-one percent of the river's run between Minneapolis, Minnesota, and Cairo, Illinois, is marked with warnings against eating the fish there. The degree of pollution in the waters running past

Tennessee has caused the state to ban commercial fishing from Memphis southward.

Some 25 percent of the nation's chemical manufacture takes place around the Mississippi as it passes through Louisiana. There, where the river is polluted by the discharges from plants manufacturing chemicals, the waters are blamed for the stunting of tree growth. One resident recalls that the region's pecan trees used to grow to heights of 65 to 70 feet and provide bountiful harvests. Now they are dwarflike in size and have lost most of their limbs.

In the midst of all the devastation, however, steps are being taken to improve the condition of the Mississippi. For one, the Monsanto chemical plant at Sauget, Illinois, has changed the way it manufactures paradichlorobenzene, the principal substance in mothballs and toilet-bowl fresheners. The company, which turns out millions of pounds of the ingredient annually, previously used a manufacturing process in which water from the river was employed to cool the substance, resulting in contaminated water. In 1989, the plant adopted a new process in which the water no longer makes contact and thus avoids contamination. The new process was adopted as part of Monsanto's plan to reduce its land and water discharges by 70 percent in 1995.

Another helpful step: The city of Memphis, Tennessee, has stopped its longtime practice of dumping 100 million gallons of raw sewage into the Mississippi each day.

COASTS IN DANGER

The pollution that has stained America's inland waterways has likewise scarred its coastlines, endangering the health of people working and seeking recreation there and threatening the survival of the marine life far out to sea.[5] Everywhere, horror stories can be heard. Here are three that rank among the worst:

Polluted beaches ranging southward from Massachusetts to New York and New Jersey were declared unsafe for swimming in the late 1980s. Accused of being the cause of the widespread contamination was sewage from both New York and New Jersey. More than 10 million tons was yearly being hauled out to sea in barges for dumping at a point about 106 miles from New York City. Ocean tides were said to be carrying it back to shore, where everything from sludge to medical wastes to drug paraphernalia was deposited.

Ships—from freighters and naval vessels to sports and commercial fishing boats—have been accused of dumping such garbage as Styrofoam eating ware, beer and soft-drink bottles and cans, and plastic bags overboard near the coasts along the Atlantic, Pacific, and Gulf of Mexico. Littering the sea, the discarded material has caused tragic harm to the life there. It is estimated to be killing as many as 100,000 sea creatures and 2 million birds per year. Among the victims are sea turtles that choke to death on plastic bags, having mistaken them for jellyfish. The damage ashore can be clearly demonstrated by just one example. In 1987, when a group of volunteers set about cleaning a stretch of Texas beach on the Gulf, they collected some 307 tons of rubbish. Among the litter were more than 31,700 plastic bags and almost 30,300 bottles.

During the late 1980s, portions of at least nine areas along the Pacific Coast—from southern California to upper Washington—were closed to the harvesting of shellfish. Eight areas along the coast were identified as containing fish with high levels of toxic industrial and household chemicals in their livers. A 1990 study of sea otters from California to Alaska revealed that, due to industrial pollution, their bodies are now housing greater levels of lead than ever before. The otters have always absorbed some lead from their natural surroundings, but today they are showing a lead content forty times that of their forebears. According to marine scientists, the increased content indicates that toxic industrial chemicals, which have long poisoned tiny organisms on the ocean floor, are now beginning to affect larger sea animals. Scientists do not yet know if the lead content has reached a level capable of killing the otters, but suspect that it may be responsible for the recent deaths of at least two of the animals.

These are just three stories of what the members of our modern society—from our industrialists to the individual who thoughtlessly tosses a soft-drink can into the sea—are doing to the nation's coastlines. But, as is true of our wetlands, lakes, and rivers, steps are being taken to correct a deplorable and highly dangerous situation.

The United States in 1988 joined twenty-eight other nations in signing an international treaty aimed at reducing ocean pollution. The pact, which went into effect in 1989, forbids all types of oceangoing craft—liners, freighters, naval ships, and fishing and pleasure boats—from dumping plastic materials into the sea.

California environmentalists have long opposed and fought the leasing of publicly owned offshore sites for oil drilling. Their objections have been many and have ranged from the charge that the offshore platforms sully the horizon to the fear that leaks and spills will blacken the coastline and sicken and kill its fish, birds, and land animals. Oil officials have countered the objections with the argument that the offshore drilling sites are necessary to help meet the nation's overwhelming need for petroleum products. At present, a number of the state's environmental groups are working to have a recently approved federal marine refuge off the coast of northern California expanded. Once established as a refuge, the area will be off-limits to oil drilling, and the groups are urging that it be expanded from a planned 2,900 square miles to some 3,800 square miles. Whether the expansion is approved or not, the new sanctuary will join those already established alongside it to give the nation its largest marine refuge—an ocean region of some 5,800 square miles.

In Washington State a program has been under way since 1985 to clear the heavily contaminated Puget Sound of industrial waste. The program to cleanse the 3,200-square-mile sound is financed in part by a surtax on the purchase of cigarettes. State and local water officials are working with industry on the development of new strategies to reduce the amount of waste matter being deposited in the sound.

There is no doubt that the nation—its people, certain of its industries, and its federal, state, and local governments—is fighting to ease the pollution staining its watery tracts. Their efforts are proving helpful. But there is also no doubt that pollution of all types—in the atmosphere, on the land, and in the waters—is outrunning the efforts to end it. We can only hope that the problem can be solved soon and do all that we can to assist in its solution. Otherwise, we will ultimately have to face the terrible question that has plagued us for years: What will become of our lands and waters, our wildlife, and ourselves?

6 OUR NATIONAL FORESTS: THEIR STORY

The harm being inflicted on the nation's watery tracts has received widespread attention in the U.S. press. But, at present, the press is giving even more attention to what is happening to our forests. It is in the forests—especially the national forests—that some of the fiercest battles in today's conflict over the American wilderness are taking place.

We begin with the steps leading to the creation of our National Forest System.

ENDLESS MILES OF TREES

When the first settlers arrived in what was to become the United States, they found themselves in a land blanketed with trees. Wherever they ventured ashore along the northern and central coasts of the Atlantic Seaboard, they sighted thick forests that stretched westward for seemingly endless miles and that, as later explorers and settlers would discover, extended over the faraway mountain ranges to the plains of the continent's midsection.

Immediately, the new arrivals put their axes and saws to the trees that clustered all about them. Trees fell to make way for the fields needed to grow crops and to provide wood for people's homes, barns, fences, and fireplaces. An era of unrestrained cutting of the eastern and northeastern timberlands—and then of those that extended all the way to the Pacific Coast—had begun.

Two ideas were behind this unrestrained cutting.[1] First, the earliest settlers came from Europe. Major portions of the forests there had been cleared away over the centuries to make way for farms and cities. For many Europeans, the farms and cities represented civilization, while the forests stood for all that was uncivilized. And, for many a European, especially the superstitious peasant, the forest was a frightening and savage place. It was there that evil creatures were to be found—the place where witches, devils, ghosts, vampires, and other harmful beings lurked. This fear, which stemmed in great part from old folktales and legends, was reflected in two of the most famous forest dwellers in fairy-tale literature—the wolf in *Little Red Riding Hood* and the evil old woman in *Hansel and Gretel*.

And so, when the first American settlers began felling the trees in their new homeland, they were doing something more than carving out farm fields and securing the material needed for building and heating their homes. They were bringing civilization—that is, their idea of civilization—to a land they saw as a dangerous wilderness, a land of untamed animals and savage native peoples. They simply did not understand that the wholesale felling of trees could disrupt all the surrounding nature, the complex of plant and animal life that we now call an ecosystem.

Nor did they understand what a Native American chief, Luther Standing Bear of the Oglala Sioux, understood—that only the white man saw nature as a wilderness. Only to the white man, the chief said, "was the land 'infested' with 'wild animals' and 'savage' people. To us it was tame. Earth was bountiful and we were surrounded with the blessing of the Great Mystery."

The second idea held by the newcomers—and those who came in their wake during the eighteenth and nineteenth centuries—was that the forests would provide the people with an inexhaustible supply of wood. With seemingly endless stretches of timberland to be seen wherever they looked, they did not stop to think that the supply of wood might be finite—that it might well disappear in time unless there was reduced cutting and by a program of planting new trees to replace those that were being lost.

These two ideas resulted in the denuding of vast stretches of the northeastern and eastern forests—especially those in the Northeast—with little or no consideration given to tree replacement or more prudent cutting practices. Then, as the nation's settlers moved ever westward, the lumber industry moved with them, venturing into the southern states and into the dense white pine forests of Minnesota, Michigan, and Wisconsin, where trees on both government and privately owned land began to topple. In time, by late in the nineteenth century, the timber industry in Michigan alone had stripped an astonishing 96 percent of Michigan's original treasure in white pine.

A GROWING SENSE OF ALARM

What the westward movement of the timber industry was doing to the nation's wilderness disturbed many Americans of the nineteenth century. They thought that the savage deforestation was destroying some of the country's most beautiful expanses and depriving it too quickly of one of its most valuable natural resources. These individuals were the first of the nation's preservationists and conservationists.

One of their number was a Vermonter named George Perkins Marsh, an energetic and multitalented man.[2] He was a linguist, an architect, a politician, and a naturalist. In his political career, Marsh served as a congressman from Vermont and as a diplomat to Turkey and Italy. But it was as a nature writer that he won his greatest fame and exerted his greatest influence on the country. In 1864, he published a book entitled *Man and Nature*. It was reissued in revised form ten years later as *The Earth as Modified by Human Action*.

In the book, Marsh lashed out at the idea that an inexhaustible supply of timber was to be had from the forests. He wrote of how he felt certain that "a desolation like that which has overwhelmed many once beautiful and fertile regions of Europe" would soon spread throughout major U.S. regions unless "prompt measures" were taken to halt the destruction being done by the logging companies.

But Marsh did more in his book than issue a warning for the future. Basing his views on what he had seen of the denuded forests in his native Vermont, he wrote of the damages to nature wrought by deforestation. He spoke of the soil erosion that soon follows the unrestrained use of the ax, and of the floods and mudslides that come when the trees are no longer there to hold the surrounding earth in place nor absorb much of the ground's water content. (We know today that one deciduous tree, when fully grown, can soak up a ton of water from the ground daily.) And he spoke of how the lives of the plants and animals in an area are disrupted—and often lost—when the trees that have sheltered and nurtured them for eons are taken away.

Marsh's book deeply affected the nation's general public and the preservationist and conservationist movements that were taking shape at the time. Hitherto, the federal government's policy had been to dispose of its public lands by leasing, selling, or giving them away for such purposes as farming, ranching, mining, and logging, to foster the growth of the young United States. The strategy had proved successful and had been supported by the people. But now, because of Marsh and the preservationist and conservationist movements, the public's attitude underwent a change. An increasing number of people began to worry about the fate of the country's wilderness. This concern helped lead to the establishment of our first national park at Yellowstone in 1872.[3]

It also opened the way to a variety of actions on behalf of the forests. In 1869, the Michigan legislature, worried and angry over the blinding speed with which its pine forests were disappearing, issued a report that said the present legislators would be condemned or lauded by future generations on the basis of whether they allowed the damage to go on unchecked or took steps to put a stop to it. Next, in 1873, the U.S. Congress passed the Timber Culture Act. The measure was aimed at encouraging people to begin planting new trees and replacing those that had been felled. It stipulated that settlers could acquire free title to 160 acres of public land by agreeing to plant and sustain trees on 40 of those acres for ten years.

In 1875, the National Forestry Association was formed to acquaint the public with the damage being done to the nation's wilderness and to press for federal legislation that would help reduce or stop the damage altogether. A year later, Congress authorized two thousand dollars for a study of the forest problem and considered a bill to set aside some wooded lands as reserves and make them safe from the logging industry. The measure was never passed, but it was revived and enacted as the Creation Act of 1891. The measure was included in a massive, congressional bill that covered many issues and was known as the General Reform Act. The Creation Act authorized the president to establish "forest reserves" on federally held lands.

THE FIRST NATIONAL FORESTS

Three presidents in turn—Benjamin Harrison, Grover Cleveland, and Theodore Roosevelt—acted on the new law and together designated 43 million acres as reserves.[4] President Harrison began by setting aside 13 million acres. Mr. Cleveland followed with 4.5 million acres, with his action much influenced by the report which, as you'll recall from chapter 2, was prepared by the national committee headed by John Muir. Theodore Roosevelt added the remaining 25.5 million acres. Most of the reserved forests were now located in the American West and Northwest. By now, the logging industry was moving in on the Pacific shores and threatening the forests of California, Oregon, and Washington.

Those 43 million acres marked the beginning of today's National Forest System, with its 191 million acres of woodlands and grasslands. At first, their management was entrusted to the General Land Office of the Department of the Interior. But, in 1905, the Forest Service of the U.S. Department of Agriculture was formed and took over the job from the General Land Office. Appointed to head the new service was a conservationist named Gifford Pinchot. He headed the service until 1910 and, during that time, influenced President Theodore Roosevelt, an ardent nature lover, to assign 148 million additional acres to the reserve program.

You'll recall that President Cleveland ran into trouble with the timber industry when he authorized the establishment of the forest reserves recommended in John Muir's report. President Roosevelt, in 1907, encountered a similar difficulty. A group of northwestern congressmen who supported the work of the timber industry in their area won passage of a bill that took away the power to establish the reserves that the General Reform Act had granted to the president. With Pinchot's help, Mr. Roosevelt, before putting his signature to the bill and turning it into law, quickly designated twenty-one new reserve areas that totaled some 17 million acres.

Mr. Roosevelt's actions in establishing the reserves were also influenced by John Muir. The president had once spent a vacation at Yosemite and had been deeply moved by the naturalist's views of nature.

A DEBATE AND ITS TWO QUESTIONS

At the time the Forest Service was created in 1905, a raging debate over the future of the reserved forests centered on two questions. First, as the preservationists urged, should the reserved lands be kept in their natural state and set aside for the public's enjoyment, as were the national parks? Or, as the conservationists recommended, should they be utilized for various purposes that were seen as productive for and needed by the American people? Should their water resources, for instance, be used for agricultural purposes? Should their meadowlands be employed as grazing grounds for the animals that provided food for so many tables? Should some of the lands be mined for oil and valuable minerals? And should portions of the forests be logged for needed wood products?

Preservationist John Muir had led the campaign that gave us our national parks. Now conservationist Gifford Pinchot, as chief of the Forest Service, became a leader in setting a different course for the national forests. With the strong support of President Theodore Roosevelt, he urged that they be utilized for the country's economic benefit but that they be always carefully and scientifically managed so that their resources were not needlessly wasted. For example, he said that the trees in the national forests should not be indiscriminately cut and that the felled trees should be replaced through replanting and natural reseeding. In this way, the trees would serve as a renewable and never-ending national treasure. He also insisted that the mineral and oil deposits on federal lands be prudently mined. They were resources that, unlike the trees and the grazing grasses in the forest meadowlands, were not renewable. They had to be thoughtfully and carefully removed so that they would last as long as possible.

In all, Pinchot held that the forests must be managed and utilized so that they provided for "the greatest good of the greatest number in the long run."

As a result of the work done by Muir and Pinchot, the nation today has two distinct types of federal lands—those that are reserved for the public's pleasure and those that can be utilized for the nation's economic benefit.

Pinchot's conservationist philosophy, which in time became known as the concept of "multiple use," has guided the National Forest Service ever since he first urged it. It permits both recreational and commercial activities in the national forests—such recreational pursuits as camping, hiking, fishing, and hunting on the one hand, and such commercial enterprises as mining, livestock grazing, oil drilling, and logging on the other.

This philosophy has enabled the national forests to enrich the nation economically and to provide us with products that have given us one of the highest standards of living in the world. At the same time, the forests have afforded outdoor pleasures for countless Americans; as you'll recall from chapter 1, the National Forest System today boasts 108,381 miles of trails, 3,338 miles of rivers, more than 4,400 campgrounds, and upward of 1,400 picnic grounds. But Pinchot's philosophy has also made many of the system's lands a part of the battleground that the American wilderness has become.

Being waged today on that battleground—in state, privately owned, and federally controlled forests—is a conflict between environmentalists and loggers over a host of issues concerning the number and kinds of trees being felled there each year.

The next chapter brings us to those issues.

7
THE FOREST CONFLICT

There are three basic issues in the forest conflict. Each issue pertains to tree-cutting in federal, state, and privately owned lands. The three are: the number of trees being cut down, the environmental damage done by the felling, and the tree-cutting being done in what are called "old-growth forests."

THE NUMBER OF TREES BEING CUT

We begin with the number of trees being felled in our federal forests.[1] For many years after the first national forests were established, little logging was done in them, with the great bulk of the country's lumber supply coming from state lands and those owned by private individuals or the timber companies. For example, in 1910 the forests gave up 500 million board feet of lumber—a mere 2 percent of the nation's lumber production. Throughout the first decades of this century, the national forests accounted for an average of only about 4 percent of America's annual wood supply.

Accounting in great part for this meager percentage was the fact that many of the initial national forest lands were located in poor timber-producing areas. They stood in regions that were more distant from transportation than were the state and privately owned lands. Hauling the felled trees to mills and thence to market was difficult and expensive and made the federal tracts unattractive to any commercial logger who might have wished to lease them from the government.

Also responsible for the modest amount of early cutting were such men as Forest Service official Aldo Leopold and Robert Marshall, a founder of the Wilderness Society. They were staunch conservationists who stressed the importance of preserving the forests and sought to keep them in as natural a state as possible. Leopold called forest preservation an act of "ecological conscience."

When Things Changed

And so, the first decades of the twentieth century saw the national forests contribute their slight 4 percent a year to the U.S. wood supply, with the rest coming from state and private forests. But things changed with World War II and the years that followed. The increased demand for wood in war production caused the felling of forest trees to double between 1939 and 1945. Then, in the postwar years, the call for lumber products became even greater—to meet the wood, paper, and pulp needs of a booming economy and, in particular, to meet the demand for homes for all the Americans who were returning from the fighting and starting their lives anew.

The demand saw a steady increase in the logging done on national forest lands. By 1952, they were yielding 6.4 billion board feet per year, a yield that came to 13 percent of the nation's total lumber output. Ten years later, they gave up 10.7 billion board feet, or 22 percent of the total American lumber output.

The National Forest System's contribution to the

nation's lumber supply has continued to grow since 1962, but not at the same rate as before. The Forest Service reports that its acreage annually produces about 12 billion board feet of lumber.

Though the annual yield is not far above what it was in 1962, environmentalists contend that it is nevertheless too great. They point out that the yield reached a peak in 1987, when 12.7 billion board feet were harvested in the forests. They add that the 1988 harvest would have been even greater had it not been for the fires that, due in part to the severe drought conditions in the nation, leveled vast tracts of federal land that could otherwise have been logged.

The environmentalists also argue that, while the overall cutting may not be much greater than it was in 1962, the felling in certain national forests has broken records in recent years. They say that, in 1988, 5.5 billion board feet were removed from nineteen forests in the U.S. Northwest alone. That amount represented upward of 20 percent more than was removed a decade earlier.

Many people believe that the Forest Service decides on the amount of wood that is cut annually and thus they blame the service for the loss of the trees. This is a mistaken belief. The amount of wood to be cut each year is set by Congress. The service then follows the mandate of Congress.

The Forest Service's reply to charges of overcutting is that its acres today provide only 13 percent of the total volume of wood harvested annually in the United States—the same percentage as in 1962—and that the great bulk of cutting is done on privately owned and state lands. In 1990, the service reported that, since the peak year of 1987, its harvests have dropped annually—to 12.6 billion board feet in 1988 and 12 billion board feet in 1989.

Reforestation

Both the Forest Service and the timber industry hold that the loss of trees on their acreage through logging is being balanced by their reforestation programs. The Forest Service says that, in keeping with the philosophy of sustained growth voiced long ago by Gifford Pinchot, it replants some 400,000 acres of its lands per year and improves the young timber on 400,000 other acres with programs aimed at reducing the damage done by such factors as competitive vegetation. Predicting that the nation's long-time demand for wood will continue to grow through the coming years, the service reports that it is preparing to meet that demand with its reforestation efforts and other activities, such as its fertilization programs and research aimed at genetic improvements that will result in stronger, more valuable trees.

For its part, the logging industry claims that it plants three new trees for every one felled, and that it has been engaged in replanting programs since 1941, when the Weyerhaeuser Company established the industry's first tree farm. The industry then points to government statistics indicating that the nation's forest acreage, both publicly and privately owned, is actually increasing. According to the statistics, the country had 664 million acres of forestland in 1952, with 610 billion cubic feet of growing stock. By 1987, due to reforestation and natural regrowth, the wooded lands were covering 728 million acres and had 756 million cubic feet of growing stock—in all, an increase of 24 percent.

ENVIRONMENTAL DAMAGE

Equaling the widespread concern over the number of fallen trees is the worry over the environmental damage resulting from the cutting. One major concern here is the method of cutting being employed in federal, state, and privately owned forests. The method is known as clear-cutting.

Clear-Cutting

There are methods of logging, such as a system known as selective cutting, that leave a number of trees standing.

But not clear-cutting.[2] As its name indicates, it takes down all the trees in its path. Then all the surrounding vegetation that stands more than twenty inches high is cut away. The cut vegetation and the other undergrowth that remain are then burned, with loggers saying that the burning, helps to replenish the land, as does a forest fire. Because of the fires, the method is often called clear-cutting and slash-burning.

Most clear-cutting is done on state and privately owned lands. The federal government limits clear-cuts to only forty acres in national forests.

There are conflicting views on the actual amount of clear-cutting being done at present. Some foresters in California claim that, because of strict state regulations, such tree-conserving methods as selective cutting are used on 90 percent of the state's privately owned forest lands, with clear-cutting limited to the remaining 10 percent. Environmental writer Harold Gilliam claims that the tree-conserving methods are bad enough—leaving as little as 25 percent of a forest still intact—but that the clear-cutting on even 10 percent of the land is even worse. Writing in a 1990 issue of the *San Francisco Chronicle* newspaper, he claims that, if clear-cutting prevails on as little as 10 percent of the state's privately owned forest lands, it yearly levels an area equal in size to the city of San Francisco—46.1 square miles, or approximately 461 square miles every ten years.

Environmentalists angrily charge that clear-cutting has posed three great hazards. First, it has completely devastated vast tracts of splendid woods, stripping them of their trees and reducing them to scarred "deserts" of blackened stumps and incinerated vegetation. These are tracts that much of the public does not realize have been devastated. This is because forest roads are often bordered by what are called viewsheds—stretches of trees that hide the carnage beyond from view. The harm can only be sighted from the air or from distant mountain peaks. The Forest Service answers this charge by pointing out that most clear-cut areas have been—or are being—reforested.

Second, clear-cutting is accused of completely disrupting a forest's ecosystem. Not only are the trees and the wildlife harbored in their limbs and bark lost, but the earth on which they stand suffers monumental damage. Here, the environmentalists echo the warnings sounded by George Perkins Marsh more than a century ago in his book *Man and Nature*. The wholesale cutting of the trees and underbrush accelerates soil erosion, mudslides, and floods because the trees and surrounding plants are no longer there to hold the ground in place with their roots and absorb so much of the earth's water content. The Forest Service replies that clear-cutting simulates a forest fire, which is nature's way of rebuilding an old and choked wooded area and thus maintaining the health of its ecosystem.

Further, there is the threat to the forest's animal life. The environmentalists charge that clear-cutting has joined a number of modern problems—air pollution, the use of pesticides and herbicides, and the encroachment of such urban developments as summer homes, resorts, and towns—in bringing a variety of wilderness species alarmingly close to extinction. At present, as you know, the U.S. Fish and Wildlife Service lists more than five hundred animals as being "endangered species." Among them is the northern spotted owl, said to be close to extinction because of the logging practices along the Pacific Coast. In the next chapter, we will be speaking more of the northern spotted owl and the role it is playing in the battle over the Pacific forests.

The Greenhouse Effect

Finally, there is the environmentalist concern that the extensive deforestation—whether it be from clear-cutting or simply too much cutting—is contributing to the international problem called the greenhouse effect, the phenomenon that is widely thought to be contributing to a gradual rise in our planet's temperature.[3] If the rise goes unchecked, environmentalists warn that it could cause the world's ice caps and glaciers to melt. The melting could lift ocean levels to the point where they could inundate continental coastlines and islands. Environmentalists also warn that the greenhouse effect could lead to an increasing number of droughts everywhere; in fact, it has already been blamed for the droughts that have plagued various areas of the world since the 1970s.

The term "the greenhouse effect" describes an action that the earth's atmosphere exerts on the rays of heat radiated to us from the sun. When they reach us, some of their heat is absorbed by the earth, while some is reradiated into the atmosphere, with a portion of it making its way back into space. But a portion is stopped by the water vapor and gases that constitute the atmosphere. They act as a barrier that reflects the heat back down to earth again. It is this reflecting action that is known as the greenhouse effect. The reflected heat adds much to our comfort. Were we without it, scientists estimate that our planet would be much cooler than it is—from 18 to 32 degrees Fahrenheit colder.

When first coming from the sun, the heat rays pass through the same atmospheric barrier. Why, then, does the barrier not catch them at that time and bounce them back into space? Some of their number are of the near-ultraviolet type and, as such, manage to slip through because they are invisible to the barrier's gases and water content. The situation, however, reverses itself when the rays are reradiated out from the earth. Now they become visible to the barrier. It stops their progress and reflects them downward.

The greenhouse effect first came into use as a term some years ago because the barrier, in catching and reflecting the outgoing rays, seems to be functioning in the same manner as the glass roof in a garden greenhouse. The roof allows the cool outside air to enter the greenhouse and then, once the air warms itself, keeps it from escaping back outdoors. Scientists, however, warn that it is technically inaccurate to compare the action of the atmospheric barrier to that of the greenhouse roof because much of the heating in the greenhouse is due to preventing cool outside air from entering the structure to mingle with and cool the air inside. Nevertheless, the term continues to be used worldwide.

The greenhouse effect has existed ever since the water vapor and gases in the atmosphere first took shape. It is considered a danger today for two reasons. First, as has happened periodically through the ages, the earth's climate seems to be undergoing a change at present. Our planet has experienced both extremely cold and extremely warm periods in its long history, with some lasting for centuries, and others remaining on the scene for just a few decades or years, and scientists have noted that the planet has embarked on a warming trend since the early 1800s. The earth's climate is now 1 degree Fahrenheit warmer than it was at the beginning of the century.

Second, the gases that join the water vapor in making up the barrier are formed here on earth and have been released into the atmosphere for eons. They are emitted by various industrial processes, automotive exhausts, and such natural occurrences as plant and animal decay and forest fires. They loom as a particular danger today chiefly because the burnings and manufacturing processes of the world's industrial societies are pouring them into the sky at such a rate that greatly strengthens the atmospheric barrier. The result is that more and more heat is being reflected to earth, thus causing the global warming trend to accelerate. Scientific predictions are that, if we continue at the present rate, the earth's temperature will rise between 3 and 9 degrees Fahrenheit, by around the years 2040 to 2050.

Just how harmful will such a rise be? At the end of the last great cold period—the Ice Age—the returning warmth raised the earth's temperature 9 degrees over a span of 10,000 years. Those few degrees melted enough ice to raise ocean levels some 250 feet. Low-lying islands disappeared and continental coastlines were drastically altered.

Of the gases in the barrier, carbon dioxide (CO_2) ranks as the most dangerous so far as the greenhouse effect is concerned. It is a colorless, odorless gas that is created when one carbon atom is mingled with two oxygen atoms. It is formed in various ways. When we breathe, we take in oxygen and exhale CO_2. Large amounts are released into the air when plant and animal bodies decompose, when fossil fuels are burned, and when trees are cut or burned. It is also used commercially in products such as carbonated drinks and fire extinguishers.

It is at this point that today's deforestation in the United States and a number of other countries comes to the forefront. Though industrial and automotive burnings of the fossil fuels are responsible for most of the carbon dioxide in the atmosphere, deforestation ranks right behind them as a troublemaker.

This is because trees are superb storehouses of carbon dioxide. They absorb and then hold great amounts of the gas in their trunks. When they are felled, they are lost as storehouses, with the carbon dioxide they would have otherwise absorbed remaining in the atmosphere. When, as is happening in many countries, they are burned, their CO_2 content rushes skyward in rolling clouds of smoke.

One of the world's most tragic deforestation programs is evident in the rain forests of South America's Amazon Basin. There, adding countless tons of carbon dioxide to the atmosphere each year, millions of acres of trees are being cut and burned to clear the land for settlement, agriculture, grazing, recreation, and oil exploration. Worldwatch Institute, an American organization engaged in the study of global environmental problems, reported alarming news from Brazil in 1988, saying that satellite data revealed that an Amazon area the size of Austria (32,266 square miles) had been burned the year before and that even larger tracts were expected to be burned in the future.

Adding to the Amazon tragedy is the fact that the rain forests there house myriad varieties of plant and animal life that are being destroyed as the trees are toppled and burned. Further, much of the cutting has gone for naught because many of the farms that were established in its wake have failed to produce abundant crops and subsequently have been abandoned.

Equally distressing word comes from the rain forests in Southeast Asia, especially those in Thailand, Burma, Cambodia, and the islands of Indonesia. Their trees are reportedly being felled at a rate of about 12,500 acres per day, implying the daily loss of countless carbon dioxide storehouses. The forests are being leveled to make way for farms and to help the Southeast Asian economies through the sale of timber. The forests on the mainland of Southeast Asia contain approximately 80 percent of the world's remaining supply of the highly valuable wood, teak. Only 10 percent of the forest lands are being replanted.

Worldwatch Institute estimates that, since 1960, deforestation worldwide has poured between 90 and 180 billion tons of carbon dioxide into the atmosphere, there to mingle with the CO_2 already in the sky and add to the greenhouse effect. That amount was joined by 150 to 190 billion tons from the automotive and industrial burnings of the fossil fuels.

While there is widespread agreement that heavy deforestation worldwide is adding to the greenhouse effect, certain claims about its hazards are subjects of disagreement among many scientists.

For one, the heat that deforestation generates has been widely blamed for the droughts that have plagued many parts of the world—the United States, Europe, Africa, and Australia among them—since the 1970s. But many scientists seriously doubt that the effect is the principal villain here. They point to other possible factors, a chief one being two giant bands of water—one exceptionally warm and the other abnormally cold—that take shape periodically in the Pacific Ocean near the equator and then spread across the ocean. They do not occur side by side in the ocean. Rather each one appears by itself, remains on the scene for about two years, and then is replaced by the other. Each triggers atmospheric disturbances that change the weather patterns in widely separated areas of the world, bringing heavy rains to some regions and severe droughts to others. The warm water band is known as El Niño, and cold water band as La Niña.

There is also doubt among some scientists that our planet's climate is still in the midst of the warming trend that began in the mid-1800s. Weather data have been collected in recent years to suggest that our climate is no longer warming but cooling instead. The data show that, after warming for about a century, the climate began to cool around 1950 and has continued to cool ever since. *But* there are also recent data indicating that a new warming trend began in the 1970s.

These contrary findings have left weather scientists facing two puzzling questions: Did the cooling that began in the 1950s mark the start of a long-lasting trend or was it simply a dip in the century-old warming trend? Did the warming that reappeared in the 1970s mark a continuation of the century-old warming trend or did it simply interrupt the cooling trend for a time? At present, since climatic changes take years to develop, there are no answers to these questions. Only time will give us the answers.

THE ATTACK ON THE OLD-GROWTH FORESTS

In great part, there was not heavy cutting in the country's early national forests because they were not of the "old-growth" type. Most old-growth forests were located on privately owned lands. They contained the most mature and, consequently, the tallest and thickest trees. Their trees were highly prized by the timber industry because of the quality of their wood and their size. They could yield twice as many board feet per acre as the younger trees in the national forests.

But, in the years since the creation of the National Forest System, many wooded areas containing old-growth trees have been added to the system. Today, the fiercest of all the battles in the wilderness conflict is being fought over the felling of old-growth stands on the nation's federal, state, and privately owned lands.

"Old growth" refers to woodlands thick with trees from hundreds of years to more than a thousand years old.[4] Environmentalists consider it criminal to cut into these forests. Being sacrificed, they charge, are the nation's most beautiful and venerable trees—trees that, reaching to heights of three hundred feet or more, are magnificent forms of life, trees that required hundreds of years to take shape, trees that support myriad plant and animal species in their branches, in their bark, and on the ground all about them. They are invaluable, irreplaceable, and beautiful life-forms and must be spared. To destroy them and take them from us is not only to destroy splendid creations but also to destroy something in our own nature and spirit. In demanding that these trees be forever spared, today's environmentalists are echoing the thoughts of one of America's foremost nature writers, Henry David Thoreau (1817–1862), when he wrote, "In wildness is the preservation of the world."

But the old-growth trees are *not* being spared. Moreover, in the eyes of environmentalists everywhere, these valuable trees are being cut at an outrageous pace. When the first colonists arrived, the land that was to become the United States was carpeted with some 850 million acres of ancient forests. At that time, some of the trees, such as the sequoia, were more than a thousand years old. Today, hundreds of thousands of acres of these woodlands are protected from logging because they have been set aside as national parks and wilderness areas. There remain little more than a million untouched acres—about 15 percent of what was here originally. They stand on federal, state, and private lands.

Most of those remaining million acres are located along the Pacific Coast. They stretch from northern California through Oregon to Washington and thence (after passing through Canada's British Columbia) to Alaska. According to environmental and Forest Service reckoning, these lands are being axed at a rate of 170 acres a day—or upward of 62,000 acres annually—a pace that could see the trees a thing of the past within a few decades. Some studies indicate that the trees *could disappear within the next fifteen years.*

Including the old-growth forests in states other than those along the Pacific, the annual loss of old-growth trees is estimated at approximately 70,000 acres. The National Audubon Society reports that every year enough of these ancient trees are cut to fill a convoy of lumber trucks 20,000 miles long. In fairness to the timber industry, however, it must be said that the world's appetite for wood products—from homebuilding materials to furniture, household decorations, toys, and fuel—is responsible for that 20,000-mile-long convoy.

Though old-growth forests have been harvested since the start of the American timber industry, their heaviest cutting coincided with the overwhelming demand for new housing in the years immediately following World War II. To meet the demand, the timber industry cut so deeply into the old-growth forests on its own lands and on acreage that it leased from private ownership that over time the old trees began to disappear. This loss caused the industry to begin leasing state and federal lands. These leases encompassed a number of newer forests and many old-growth woodlands.

The leasing and cutting of old-growth forests on federal as well as state and private lands continue to this day. Environmentalists charge that the cutting, unless stopped by new laws and public pressure, will continue until all the trees are gone, because their wood garners such a profit. Clear-cutting, the environmentalists further say, is adding to the problem by hastening the rate at which the forests are being denuded. (Proponents of clear-cutting argue that it is serving the American people by helping to keep the price of wood products down. Their price tag would rise if less wood were available.) Surveys and environmental studies show that the old-growth stands on privately owned lands have all but disappeared in California and elsewhere.

The claims by forest officials and timber industry representatives that replanting programs are replacing and even expanding the nation's woodlands fall on deaf environmentalist ears when it comes to the old-growth forests. The environmentalists feel that the replanted forests, with their trees all of the same age and the same height, cannot possibly match the varied scenic wonders, the majestic primordial beauty, and diversity of wildlife found in the old-growth forests. If left untouched after being felled, today's old-growth forest will need a thousand years to restore itself and provide visitors once again with its natural splendors.

An Opposing View

Not everyone, however, agrees that the replanted forests will fail in their beauty and the value of their wood. Economics journalist Warren T. Brookes believes that the environmentalists have gone too far. He accuses them of thinking that the only good tree is an old tree. He defends the replanted forests by pointing to Sweden.

Writing in an April 1990 column, Brookes reported that Sweden was a tree-barren land with just a few forests in the mid-nineteenth century. But then the Swedish government embarked on a program to promote both the planting and harvesting of trees. Since 1905, as has long been the policy in the United States, Swedish loggers have been required to plant three new trees for every tree cut. The replacement must take place within three years of the cutting.

Today, Sweden is a land rich in forests, and supports thriving lumber, paper, and pulp industries. In his column, Brookes quoted Jan Remrod, the director of the Swedish Association of Forest Industries, as saying that most of the country's forests are planted by human hands and not an act of nature. Remrod is further quoted as stating that 75 percent of Sweden's forests are in private hands and that, because cutting and reforestation keep pace with each other, the trees have become a constant national resource that is never fully consumed.

The Canadian Problem

The United States does not stand alone in being accused of the wholesale destruction of old-growth forests. Western Canada is also coming under heavy environmentalist fire.[5]

Logging has always been a major industry in Canada, with lumber being much in demand for export and for domestic fuel and construction. The forests that have been cut in the country's eastern provinces have long been the objects of replanting programs.

At present, however, the logging practices in British Columbia, Canada's westernmost province, are being severely criticized. There, in 1989 alone, loggers cut nearly 600,000 acres of public forestlands, a total that far exceeded the public acreage harvested in the United States. Hit by clear-cutting were old-growth forests that are extensions of the forests stretching up the Pacific Coast from northern California. Stands of ancient firs, cedars, and Sitka spruce were harvested. Some of the cedars were more than a thousand years old, while a number of the spruce stood more than three hundred feet tall and were revered as being among the biggest trees in the world.

The right to harvest the forests was granted to commercial loggers by British Columbia's provincial government. This brought complaints from environmentalists throughout Canada and the United States and from such distant points as Great Britain and New Zealand. All demanded that the cutting be curtailed and expressed the fear that, if the savaging continued at the 1989 rate, most of the British Columbia forests would disappear in a generation. Even a number of the loggers involved in the cutting, though they risked losing their jobs should it be curtailed or banned altogether, were upset by the sacrifice of the magnificent trees and by the rate at which they were falling.

Much of the anger stemmed from the fact that the British Columbia forests are rain forests that absorb moisture from the clouds and help to give the region its cool climate. The loss of the forests could result in a dramatic change of climate and could likewise contribute to a heightening of the greenhouse effect.

There was also anger at the profit motive behind the cutting. Many charged that the forests were being sacrificed so that their wood could be exported to a number of Asian countries, Japan among them, that are currently buying vast quantities of North American timber to satisfy their building and manufacturing needs. In chapter 9, we will talk more of the anger that the foreign thirst for lumber is causing among Canadians and also among Americans, environmentalists, and loggers alike.

Canadian timber companies have always faced fewer restrictions than their counterparts in the United States. For example, as mentioned earlier, clear-cutting in U.S. national forests is limited to forty acres, while no such limit exists in Canada. However, in the wake of the 1989 cutting, a majority of the 3 million people in British Columbia have voiced a desire to see new restrictions placed on the logging practices there. A law recently went into effect that requires the British Columbia loggers to undertake replanting programs. At the same time, the province took steps to protect from further harm one of the regions hardest hit by the loggers. It set aside half of the small but richly forested Carmanah Valley as a park. The 16,500-acre valley is located on the southwestern coast of Vancouver and today boasts some of the world's largest spruce trees.

While environmentalists are concerned about the fate of all the nation's outdoors, the battle of the American wilderness is at its fiercest in the old-growth forests. Let us now see what is happening there.

8
THE BATTLE OVER THE OLD-GROWTH FORESTS

The battle over the old-growth forests is a complex one that is being fought along three main fronts: in the forests themselves, in the political arena, and in the voting booth.

IN THE FORESTS

Here, the battle has brought environmentalists face-to-face with the men and women—and their families—who depend directly on the timber industry for their livelihoods. It is especially a sore point for the loggers who see their jobs as being threatened by the environmental movement. But no environmentalist or environmental organization has triggered as much ill feeling as the group known as "Earth First."

Earth First

Earth First (officially, the group uses an exclamation mark at the end of its name—Earth First!) is a nationwide organization of militant environmentalists whose strategy is to infiltrate the old-growth forests and hamper logging operations.[1] In 1989, the group created national headlines when its members attempted to delay timber operations in six states—Washington, Oregon, California, Montana, Colorado, and New Mexico.

One Earth First band in Washington climbed some sixty feet up three trees that were scheduled to be felled that day in the Mount Baker–Snoqualmie National Forest. The Earth Firsters settled down with a week's supply of food on small plywood platforms that they had hoisted into the branches. From their perches, they defied the loggers to put chain saws to the trees and unfurled signs reading: FORESTS, NOT FRAGMENTS and SAVE AMERICA'S FORESTS. At the same time, a fellow group blocked a logging road in northern California, an action that resulted in a brawl between the group members and local loggers. A small band in New Mexico temporarily halted tree-cutting on a hillside by chaining themselves to logging machinery.

Though these tactics earned national headlines, another of Earth First's strategies has made the group even more famous—actually, "infamous" is a more accurate word because the tactic has been angrily condemned not only by loggers but by the general public and most environmentalists as well. The strategy, which the group used for several years, is known as tree spiking. It calls for long metal spikes to be driven into the trunks of trees in the logger's path. The spikes do not harm the trees themselves, but are a proven danger to the machinery in sawmills and, worse, to the millworkers. When struck by a mill blade, a spike shatters and destroys the blade. Three workers at a sawmill in the northern California town of Cloverdale were killed in 1987 when a blade shattered on grinding its way into a spike.

In April 1990, the northern California branch of Earth First issued a statement in which it announced that its members were abandoning the use of spiking. The statement said that spiking was being dropped because of requests by timber company employees who shared the group's concern for the number of old-growth trees being cut and who feared being injured or killed while on their jobs.

In part, the statement read: "The loggers and mill workers are our neighbors, and they should be our allies, not our adversaries." One of the group members told the press that the statement came in the wake of an Oregon meeting with timber employees. He said that one logger had branded tree spiking a cowardly act that endangered the lives of mill workers. The Earth Firster went on to say that his group believes the environment cannot be saved without the help of the timber employees. Those employees, he added, need to feel that the environmental movement is on their side. Tree spiking prevents them from doing so.

Earth First's stated reasons for abandoning the spiking earned a scornful reaction from timber industry representatives. They contended that the move was not inspired by the desire to save lives but by the adverse publicity that Earth First had received in the press since the deaths of the three Cloverdale workers in 1987 and by the anger and shock that spiking had triggered in other environmentalists and the general public.

Though declaring that they themselves were renouncing tree spiking, the northern California Earth Firsters pointed out that they were not denouncing its use by fellow activist groups or their own organization elsewhere in the nation. Nor, according to one member, was the California contingent abandoning its other confrontational tactics, a claim that was proved in August and September of 1990.

Redwood Summer

During those two months, the branch joined several environmental groups in sponsoring what was called Redwood Summer, a series of protests against the logging of ancient redwoods in northern California. The participants staged antilogging demonstrations in various lumber towns, among them Eureka, Fort Bragg, and Fortuna. The demonstrations involved bands of activists that ranged in size from a dozen or so to upward of a thousand and brought them face-to-face with angry loggers.

The largest demonstrations were held at Fort Bragg and Fortuna, with the former involving some 1,500 activists, and the latter approximately 600. At Fortuna, the demonstrators marched onto the grounds of the Pacific Lumber Company's mill. Pacific Lumber was chosen as a target because the company had been purchased by the Maxxom Corporation in 1987 and, to pay off the $750-million cost of the acquisition, had since outraged environmentalists by doubling—tripling, according to some estimates—its lumber output.

As they entered the company grounds, the demonstrators passed between ranks of some four hundred loggers, their families, and friends. Angry words were exchanged. But fortunately there was no outbreak of violence. The demonstration was watched and controlled by two hundred riot-control police officers, who had been brought in from various points in northern California to keep the peace.

There is widespread agreement among environmentalists and loggers that Earth First's confrontational and militant tactics have done little or no good in resolving the old-growth forest conflict. On the other hand, there is at least one example in which quiet discussions between environmentalists and loggers have resulted in what many people see as a beginning solution to the conflict. The example comes from the small Montana logging town of Libby.

The Libby Agreement

In August 1990, just prior to the start of Redwood Summer out in California, a group consisting of environmentalists from the Montana Wilderness Association and representatives from the local labor union of loggers sat down and reached a decision concerning the future of the 2.2-million-acre Kootenai National Forest.[2] The forest was being heavily logged, and the two groups agreed that it should be divided into two sectors—one designated as timberland for logging and the other designated as a wilderness area to be henceforth rendered safe from the chain saw.

Actually, only a small percentage of the Kootenai land—about 2 percent—was set aside as a wilderness area. But the agreement was seen as significant because it came about through negotiations rather than confrontations between two warring camps. It could well serve as a guide for similar actions in other areas.

In fact, it quickly succeeded in doing just that. A few days after the Kootenai pact, another group of environmentalists and loggers agreed to set aside 750,000 acres in southwestern Montana's Lolo National Forest and protect them from timber felling. Both the Kootenai and Lolo agreements have yet to be enacted into law by Congress.

ON THE POLITICAL FRONT

On the political front, one of the most important figures in the old-growth forests conflict is neither an environmentalist nor a logger. Rather, it is a feathered animal that weighs around twenty-two ounces and stands a mere fourteen inches or so tall—the chocolate-colored and round-eyed creature known as the northern spotted owl. The owl has become a weapon in the hands of the environmentalists in their efforts to save the old-growth forests.

The Northern Spotted Owl

The spotted owl's role in the forest battle can be traced to 1973 when the U.S. Congress, worried over the number of animal species being rendered extinct by modern industrial, recreational, and housing developments, enacted the Endangered Species Act.[3] The act, as you'll recall from chapter 5, makes it a federal crime for any activity to threaten the survival of any animal species by disturbing its habitat.

Under the provisions of the act, the construction of the Tellico Dam in Tennessee was halted in the late 1970s because environmentalists contended that it was jeopardizing the existence of the snail darter, a tiny fish three inches long. The construction ban lasted for two years. It was finally lifted when Congress declared the dam exempt from the act and after the little snail darter was removed from the area and successfully transplanted elsewhere.

The northern spotted owl came to the forefront of the forest battle in the late 1980s. At that time, environmentalists began to charge that the little animal, which is found mainly in old-growth forests, was fast becoming extinct because of the intense logging being done along the Pacific Coast. They estimated that only 1,700 pairs of spotted owls remained in the old-growth forests, a decline of more than half their population since the early 1800s. The owl is a slow-breeding animal and the environmentalists claimed that it would take an astonishing one hundred years for its number to increase to 2,200 pairs.

In 1989, the U.S. Fish and Wildlife Service (FWS), at the behest of various environmental organizations, undertook a study of the owl. The service, which, in keeping with the Endangered Species Act, maintains a list of animals threatened with extinction, said that it would issue a report on the study in mid-1990. The report would recommend whether the owl should be placed on the Endangered Species List; if so, a plan for its protection would have to be devised by the federal government. Contrary to the environmentalist estimate, the FWS figured that approximately 4,500 northern spotted owls remained in the Pacific Coast's old-growth forests.

At the time the FWS study began, the U.S. government calculated that, were the owl to be listed as endangered, the protection of its habitat could possibly close some 3 million federal acres along the Pacific to logging. Considering the small number of owls said to be alive, this amount seemed especially great to many Americans. The calculation, however, was based on the fact that the owl does not reside in a single tree. It requires a large area in which to forage for prey. Each foraging area, as part of the animal's habitat, would need to be protected.

The chance that the owl would be declared an endangered species triggered a flurry of activity by the environmentalists. On the little creature's behalf, a number of their organizations—among them the Sierra Club—went to court and obtained injunctions (orders) against the logging activities in certain wooded areas where it was to be found. The injunctions reduced the amount of timber available for cutting on public and private forests lands in 1989 from 5.4 billion board feet to 2.4 billion board feet.

The Pacific Coast timber companies reacted with anger to all that was happening. Should the FWS study result in the owl being placed on the Endangered Species List, the companies said that the estimated loss of 3 million federal acres would reduce timber production by more than a third. They predicted that up to 30,000 of their employees would be put out of work and that the shortage of lumber would damage the economy of the entire country by driving up the price of wood products for the American consumer.

Anger ran especially high in Oregon, where the logging and wood products industry brings in $7 billion a year and provides employment for 150,000 people. The state's timber companies and their employees felt certain that, once the owl was listed as endangered, their industry would be devastated. Workers took to wearing T-shirts emblazoned with the words SAVE A LOGGER, EAT AN OWL, and I LOVE OWL—FRIED. The Oregon anger ran even higher after the environmental groups obtained the injunctions that reduced the amount of timber available for harvest in 1989. Of the Pacific forests, Oregon's were the hardest hit by the injunctions.

(Ironically, in October 1990, *The Oregonian* newspaper reported that, even without the spotted owl problem, the annual timber harvests in the northwest forests were destined to be reduced—this because the forests had been overcut through the years and not enough new trees had sprouted or been planted back in the 1950s.)

With a major segment of the state's economy in jeopardy, a number of Oregon environmentalists, loggers, and political figures met in the summer of 1989 to work out a forest harvest plan that would be fair to both the environmental and logging sides of the issue. They hammered out a plan, intended to remain in effect until the FWS completed its study in 1990, which called for some old-growth areas to be logged while others would be left alone for the protection of the spotted owl. The plan also prohibited anyone from seeking court injunctions against further cutting.

The timber industry accepted the plan, but the environmentalists turned it down and voiced a particular dislike for the provision banning efforts to obtain court injunctions. Nevertheless, despite this disagreement, Oregon Senator Mark Hatfield took the plan to the U.S. Congress and sought its enactment into law.

There, it was strongly supported by the timber industry and just as strongly opposed by the Sierra Club, the Wilderness Society, the National Audubon Society, and other environmental organizations. As a result, Congress developed a compromise plan that was put into effect for a year. The compromise recognized the old-growth forests as national ecological treasures and, to protect the spotted owl, reduced the amount of timber that could be felled on federal old-growth lands to between 10 and 20 percent below the amount the Forest Service had approved for cutting in 1989.

The Spotted Owl Study

Meanwhile, the spotted owl study was being carried out by scientists from the Forest Service, the National Park Service, the U.S. Bureau of Land Management, and the FWS itself. In April 1990, they issued a report indicating that the owl was indeed an endangered animal and recommended that logging be banned in 30 to 40 percent of the Pacific Coast's federally owned old-growth acres.

Those acres—if converted into a series of preserves for the owl—would be lost to logging. The preserves were to be called Spotted Owl Habitat Conservation Areas. Each was to be large enough to accommodate the wide-ranging foraging travels of twenty breeding pairs of owls. The scientists also recommended that the spaces between the areas be somewhat narrow—no more than twelve miles wide—so that the owls could easily migrate from one area to another.

Because of variations in the owl population along the Pacific Coast, the scientists said that the proposed areas would differ in size. They were to range from as few as 100 acres in some California regions to as many as 600,000 in Washington's Olympic National Forest. In all, the scientists recommended that ninety-nine conservation habitats be established in California, forty-eight in Oregon, and forty-three in Washington.

Once the recommendations were made, the federal government figured that the proposed plan would cost timber workers a number of jobs, but not the 30,000 predicted by the industry. The jobs expected to be lost were variously estimated to run between 9,000 and 13,000 over a ten-year period.

It came as no surprise when the recommendations outraged the timber companies. They claimed that, if the recommendations were enacted into law, up to 25 percent of the total lumber harvest along the Pacific Coast would be lost to them. Timber harvests in the federal forests there would plunge by about 50 percent. The companies continued to insist vehemently that the reduction would eventually cost up to 30,000 logging workers their jobs.

On the Endangered Species List

On the basis of the study, the FWS placed the northern spotted owl on the Endangered Species List in June 1990. But that did not end the matter. Now, using the study recommendations as guidelines but not as provisions that must necessarily be obeyed, the federal government faced the task of working out a method that would accomplish two ends: safeguard the owl and, at the same time, provide protections for an industry that supplied jobs for thousands of people and brought a needed product to the country.

Toward this end, President George Bush, expressing concern for the welfare of the timber workers, immediately assigned the job of working out the needed method to a task force made up of members of his cabinet; key among them were Secretary of the Interior Manuel Lujan and then Secretary of Agriculture Clayton Yeutter. In September, the task force members brought a one-year plan to Congress. They advised a reduction in the old-growth cutting on some federal acreage, but indicated that Congress should not go along with the recommendations of the FWS study to ban cutting on 30 to 40 percent of the government's Pacific lands. Their advice was to shrink the amount of cutting to 14 percent below that planned for 1989.

The task force members admitted that their plan was meant to strike a new balance between the needs of the owl and the timber industry in the hope of saving some 21,000 logging and sawmill jobs in the long run.

THE BALLOT BOX

Listing the owl as an endangered species prompted California to develop a set of regulations aimed at protecting the animal by limiting the amount of old-growth cutting that could be done on both state and privately owned lands. But, for average Californians, the forest conflict was most keenly felt when it spilled into the voting booth in the November 1990 state elections. Placed on the ballot for voter rejection or approval at that time were three measures having to do with California's forests. They were:

Environment. Public Health Bonds Act. *Nicknamed "Big Green" by the voters, this environmental proposal called for a widespread attack on the various substances—from pesticides and chemicals to automobile fumes and offshore oil spills—that are threatening the air and land and water resources in one of the nation's most polluted states. It also contained a clause that called for $300 million to be spent on the acquisition and protection of old-growth forests.*

Forest Acquisition. Timber Harvesting Practices Bond Act. *An environmentalist measure, this one earned the nickname "Forests Forever" from its supporters. The proposed act called for the banning of clear-cutting on most forest lands —public and private alike—and authorized the state to spend $742 million to purchase and preserve virgin redwood forests slated for cutting. In addition, it prohibited the state from purchasing wood or timber products from companies that obtained their wood from firms that exported logs to foreign mills for processing. Further, it called for funds to be set aside to retrain for other work the timber industry employees who would lose their jobs due to the state acquisition of the forest lands.*

Forestry Programs. Timber Harvesting Practices Bond Act. *This measure, which was sponsored by the timber industry, was developed to counteract the provisions in the "Forests Forever" act. It was given two nicknames during the months prior to the election, with its supporters calling it "New Forestry" and its opponents dubbing it "Big Stump." The act required timber companies with more than 5,000 acres to prepare long-range logging and wildlife management plans. It prohibited clear-cutting in privately owned forests, but* *allowed the cutting of all trees on these lands over a period of three years. The act also required the state to study the effects of forests on global warming, and prohibited the state from buying any redwood timberlands unless the owner wishes to sell.*

All three measures triggered a statewide debate during the months before the November election. In the end, they were defeated at the polls, in great part because, at a time when the United States seemed to be entering a period of economic recession, they involved very heavy expenditures of public moneys for the purchase of the forestlands and for programs to retrain loggers for other jobs. Voters also apparently agreed with the arguments that had been leveled against the measures during the preelection months.

For example, the timber industry and other opponents of the "Big Green" measure argued that it was a hodgepodge bill trying to do the impossible—that is, cure all of the state's environmental problems in one stroke. They contended that the measure would be too clumsy for enforcement, that the costs of enforcement would be astronomical, and that it would wreak havoc on the state's various industries—logging among them—and their employees.

"Forests Forever" was denounced by the timber industry on the grounds that it would deprive thousands of logging employees of their jobs and seriously hamper the flow of wood products needed by the public. Many logging workers, however, favored one aspect of the bill—the provision that would bar the state from buying wood products from any company that obtained its wood from firms that export their logs to foreign countries for milling.

This was a slap at the Asian nations—Japan, China, Korea, and Taiwan—that have been recently buying vast quantities of uncut logs from the United States and Canada and then taking them home for cutting in their own mills. It is a practice that has caused a number of Pacific sawmills to close for want of work. Most of the anger is directed against Japan, which is buying some two-thirds of the uncut logs.

The Asian demand for uncut logs is growing, with much anger now also being directed at several major U.S. timber companies that are taking advantage of the rising demand to turn a large profit. In 1989, logs that eventually produced 4.6 million board feet of lumber were exported to the Orient. American timber workers contend that some 17,000 new jobs would be created if the companies would have those logs cut in domestic mills—or if the federal government put pressure on them to do so. The new jobs would far outnumber those that were due to be lost if the plan proposed by the FWS study group had been adopted.

Most of the shipments of uncut logs come from state and privately owned forests. The U.S. government has banned the export of uncut logs from federal lands ever since 1973. At present, the states of Oregon and Washington are working with Congress to enact legislation that would ban the export of raw logs from state lands.

As for the "New Forestry" or "Big Stump" measure, it earned nothing but scorn from the environmentalists. They tagged as ridiculous the idea of prohibiting clear-cutting on privately owned lands while at the same time allowing all the trees on these same lands to be felled in a matter of three years. They felt that that approach was doing nothing to stop clear-cutting, but simply delaying it for a short period of time.

The old-growth forests have been with us for centuries. In recent years, they have been a battleground in the conflict over the American outdoors. We turn from them now to one of the newest of the battlegrounds—the nation's wilderness areas.

9
OUR WILDERNESS AREAS: THE NEWEST BATTLEGROUND

Wilderness areas are wild and often remote regions that the U.S. Congress has set aside so that the nature and wildlife there can be preserved in as pristine a state as possible.[1] They may be used by the public for camping, hiking, backpacking, fishing, and—in certain cases—hunting. But they are kept free of roads (other than those needed for emergency purposes), buildings, and most commercial activities, with livestock grazing being an exception. The use of motorized equipment within their boundaries is forbidden. The banned equipment includes cars, trucks, recreational vehicles, motorboats, and motorcycles. Aircraft may not land in wilderness areas.

At present, as you'll recall from chapter 1, there are 474 wilderness areas (which are also known simply as wildernesses) in the United States. Covering some 90.7 million acres, they are found in forty-four states. Most are located within the boundaries of national parks and forests and on lands supervised by the U.S. Bureau of Land Management.

The greatest number of wilderness areas are housed within the National Forest System—365 of the total 474. These are found in thirty-six states and embrace some 32.5 million acres, an expanse roughly the size of Alabama. The Forest Service says that wilderness areas take up one out of every six acres in the system.

Vast wilderness tracts are also found in the National Park System. In Alaska's Kobuk Valley National Park of 1.7 million acres, some 190,000 are designated as wilderness areas. Florida's Everglades National Park devotes about 1.3 million of its nearly 1.4 million acres to wilderness. In Texas, wilderness areas take up more than half the 86,418 acres that make up the Guadalupe Mountains National Park—46,850 in all.

Hunting and livestock grazing are prohibited in the wildernesses that lie within the National Park System.

Wilderness areas vary greatly in size. The smallest is in Ohio—a tract of a mere 77 acres. Alaska, with a total of 56.49 million acres, boasts the largest amount of wilderness acreage.

The table beginning on this page lists by state the numbers of acres that Congress has set aside as wilderness areas over the years. Heading the list are the eleven states containing the largest tracts.

STATE	WILDERNESS AREAS DESIGNATED BY U.S. CONGRESS
Alaska	56.49 million acres
Arizona	2.04 million
California	5.93 million
Colorado	2.65 million
Florida	1.42 million
Idaho	4.00 million
Montana	3.44 million

New Mexico	1.61 million
Oregon	2.09 million
Washington	4.25 million
Wyoming	3.09 million

Alabama	33,396 acres
Arkansas	128,362
Georgia	460,215
Hawaii	142,370
Illinois	4,050
Indiana	12,935
Kentucky	18,056
Louisiana	17,046
Maine	7,386
Massachusetts	2,420
Michigan	248,724
Minnesota	804,489
Mississippi	7,300
Missouri	70,860
Nebraska	12,735
Nevada	64,667
New Hampshire	102,932
New Jersey	10,341
New York	1,363
North Carolina	109,003
North Dakota	39,652
Ohio	77
Oklahoma	22,525
Pennsylvania	9,705
South Carolina	60,539
South Dakota	74,074
Tennessee	66,714
Texas	81,196
Utah	802,189
Vermont	58,539
Virginia	169,453
West Virginia	80,361
Wisconsin	43,988

These many protected regions resulted from congressional passage of "An Act to Establish a National Wilderness Preservation System for the Permanent Good of the Whole People, and for Other Purposes."[2] The measure, now simply called the Wilderness Act, was passed by the Senate and House of Representatives on September 3, 1963, and was signed into law by President Lyndon B. Johnson.

In the act, Congress established the criteria by which regions have since been placed within the Wilderness Preservation System:

> *A wilderness, in contrast with those areas where man and his own works dominate the landscape, is hereby recognized as an area where the earth and its community of life are untrammeled by man, where man himself is a visitor who does not remain. An area of wilderness is further defined to mean in this Act an area of undeveloped Federal land retaining its primeval character and influence, without permanent improvements or human habitation, which is protected and managed so as to preserve its natural conditions and which (1) generally appears to have been affected primarily by the forces of nature, with the imprint of man's work substantially unnoticeable; (2) has outstanding opportunities for solitude or a primitive and unconfined type of recreation; (3) has at least five thousand acres of land or is of sufficient size as to make practicable its preservation and use in an unimpaired condition; and (4) may also contain ecological, geological, or other features of scientific, educational, or historical value.*

An Early Struggle

The 1963 passage of the act marked the end of a long struggle between environmentalists and members of Congress supported by timber, oil, mining, and grazing interests. For more than two decades, environmentalists such as the Sierra Club's David Brower urged its passage, all the while expressing the fear that federally held lands were being steadily destroyed by the various commercial activities permitted under the multiple-use concept. The commercial interests, as did those in the forest conflict, argued that their loss of federal multiple-use lands would threaten the livelihoods of thousands of Americans and severely damage the nation's economy.

For years, the pressure applied by the commercial interests prevailed in Congress and blocked any effort to have the act passed. By 1963, however, Americans everywhere were more deeply worried than ever by the relentless worsening of the nation's environment. In response to that concern—and because it was likewise shared by many senators and representatives—Congress at last enacted the measure.

Actually, prior to the act's passage, some 14 million federal acres were being protected by the government in much the same way as the wilderness areas were to be. Located mostly within the National Forest System, they were designated as primitive areas, with the first of their number being today's Gila Wilderness, which was set aside for protection in 1924. The Wilderness Act was to add mightily to their number.

Immediately following the passage of the act, 9.1 million acres in the national forests were named for wilderness status. In the years since, more than 80 million acres have joined the system, bringing it to its present 90.7 million acres.

A NEW BATTLEGROUND

A current wilderness study by the Bureau of Land Management (BLM) has turned vast tracts in the American West into the latest battleground in the conflict over the future of the nation's outdoors.[3]

Established by Congress in 1946, the BLM was given the task of managing a number of commercial enterprises, among them grazing on public lands in the West. In 1976, Congress ordered the bureau to study its land holdings with an eye toward recommending which of their number should be placed within the Wilderness System. The bureau's final recommendations were scheduled to go to the President for consideration in the early 1990s. He was to study the recommendations and then, with possible additions and subtractions, pass them on to congress for enactment into law.

The lands being studied encompass some 250 million acres in the western states of the lower forty-eight states. They boast a dazzling array of natural wonders—deserts, mountains, grasslands, volcanic craters, rivers, and lakes. Living within their boundaries are seemingly endless varieties of plant and animal life. Among the animals are elk, bears, sheep, desert tortoises, snakes, bighorn sheep, and such birds as hawks and eagles. Some of these lands are now used for commercial and recreational purposes while others remain relatively untouched.

In 1980, four years after launching its study, the BLM issued a preliminary report that stated it had selected areas covering 25 million of its acres in the western states as possible locations for designation as wildernesses. These areas met the criteria stipulated in the Wilderness Act for such a designation: They were undeveloped, were devoid of tourist accommodations and roads, and promised to give any visitor many a chance for solitude and primitive outdoor activities. The BLM now had to select which of those areas it would finally recommend to the President for wilderness status.

It was the BLM's preliminary report that turned vast tracts of our western land into the newest of the battlegrounds in the ongoing conflict over the fate of the American outdoors. Pitted against each other are the same forces that are at odds in the nation's forests—on the one side, the environmentalists and, on the other, a variety of industrial and recreational interests.

But why exactly have these western tracts become a battleground? For one thing, there is anger in the environmental camp that the BLM has pinpointed only 25 million out of 250 million acres as potential wildernesses. The BLM chose only 1.9 million acres out of 22.1 million in Utah; 1 out of 12.2 million in Arizona; and 2.3 out of 17.1 million in California. Environmentalists argue that at least three times the pinpointed total of 25 million should be considered for wilderness status.

In all, the environmentalists contend that as much acreage as possible must be set aside to safeguard untouched land from the damage already done to multiple-use tracts by commercial interests—from the awful scars that strip mining, for example, has left on the Montana landscape, and from the stretches of Utah forests that have had their trees uprooted by bulldozers moving along with chains stretched between them, all for the purpose of clearing the land for grazing. The harms wrought by strip mining, which is done with equipment that tears up the surface of the earth, has caused Montana to pass a law now requiring strip miners to repair the land after they have finished with it. This was done to prevent the mining operations from leaving behind giant heaps—literally hills—of overturned earth and great slashes in the ground.

On the opposite side of the fence, factions representing commercial and recreational interests argue that the BLM's preliminary report threatens to close too many acres to them. They are also fearful that Congress, upon receiving the final recommendations from the president in the 1990s, will want to consider adding additional regions as possible wilderness sites. These factions are pressuring their congressional supporters to come up with bills that will prevent the Senate and the House of Representatives from doing so.

The antiwilderness forces are made up of several

major contingents. Among them are housing developers who say that an increasing number of Americans are fleeing the cities and settling in more remote and peaceful areas. The BLM lands may well be needed for the building of new housing tracts and even new towns in the future. Other major groups come from the timber, mining, agricultural, and ranching interests. Such groups argue that the BLM lands should remain open for multiple use because of the needed products they provide and for the jobs they create.

Still another contingent is made up of the recreational-motor enthusiasts. They oppose the establishment of wilderness areas because it will ban them and their vehicles—their campers, dune buggies, motorcycles, and snowmobiles—from vast tracts that they are now using for outdoor fun.

The activities of the motor enthusiasts have long infuriated environmentalists across the country. Their blistering anger centers on the damage that motorized equipment has left behind over the years—for instance, the harms done by snowmobiles to the snow-covered vegetation and ground in the wooded areas of such states as Wisconsin, Michigan, and Minnesota; and the landscape wounds that motorcycles and other off-road vehicles have inflicted on sections of the desert region that covers some 25 million acres in southern California. There, the desert floor has been crisscrossed and ripped by tire tracks, an especially serious type of damage because deserts are known to heal slowly from overuse. As proof, the environmentalists point to the tracks that remain from World War II when a part of the desert was used for tank training.

The environmentalists also charge that the motor enthusiasts have stolen or marred many of the desert's ancient and irreplaceable Indian artifacts, among them rocks ornamented with long-ago carvings and paintings. As mentioned in the beginning of this book, the environmental movement would like to see damaging motorized activities everywhere banned. For their part, the motor enthusiasts argue that, as taxpayers, they have the right to pursue their activities on publicly owned lands. They are supported in their contention by the manufacturers of motorized vehicles and allied equipment.

Legislative Actions

The BLM's preliminary report led to a number of actions over the years by federal legislators interested in seeing certain lands set aside as wildernesses:

> *In 1988, Senator Alan Cranston of California offered to Congress his Desert Protection Act. The measure called for 6.5 million acres in the southern California desert to be designated as a wilderness area. The bill died in Congress, principally because of stiff opposition by mining interests in the mineral-rich area. The senator may reintroduce the bill for congressional consideration sometime in the future.*
>
> *In late 1989, Congress approved a Nevada measure to declare 733,000 acres in the state's national forests a wilderness area.*
>
> *As this book is written, Representative Wayne Owens of Utah is considering the possibility of introducing a bill aimed at protecting 5.1 million acres of BLM lands in his state by having them set aside as a wilderness. His office reports that he is discussing the measure with congressional colleagues, the BLM, and his constituents.*

WHAT THE FUTURE HOLDS FOR THE WILDERNESS AREAS

As this book is written, the BLM is completing its recommendations. They will be passed on to the president by the secretary of the interior. The president will have up to two years to consider and adjust them before sending them to Congress for action. When Congress receives the final recommendations, our federal legislators undoubtedly will have to face a number of questions, all of them critical to the future of the country's Wilderness Areas. Should *more* acreage than that advised by the president be designated as wildernesses? Or should *less* acreage be approved? How much damage will the American outdoors sustain if insufficient space is approved? How many jobs will be lost—and how much will the nation's economy suffer—if Congress decides to set aside as wildernesses the 25 million acres that the BLM report of 1980 designated as suitable for the purpose?

Only time will give us the answers.

Just as Congress faces questions triggered by the BLM's recommendations, we also face a major question as we close this book.

It is a question of balance. In light of all that we have discussed, there can be little doubt that the conflict over the fate of the American wilderness cannot be settled unless we can strike a balance between the views of the environmentalists and those of the conservationists and commercial interests. Both sides are dedicated to their own strong feelings and beliefs.

On the one hand, from the environmentalists' point of view, we need to help protect and preserve as many of the nation's natural wonders as possible—our forests, meadows, rivers, lakes, and coastlines—so that they can go on providing the enjoyment and spiritual refreshment that millions of Americans have long derived from them.

On the other hand, from the conservationists' viewpoint, we must understand that the American wilderness abounds in resources that are needed for the nation's economic well-being. When carefully and scientifically utilized, such resources can serve us now and in the future. For instance, our forests and grazing lands can be constantly renewed through replanting and natural reseeding so that they will never disappear, and our mineral and oil deposits can be slowly and prudently depleted so that they last as long as possible.

And, speaking for the conservationists and commercial interests, we need to understand that these resources provide us with products—ranging from basic building materials, necessary foods, and the minerals and oil required by our industries and transportation systems, to the most frivolous of conveniences—that contribute mightily to the nation's (and the world's) economy, make so many of our jobs possible, and afford us a standard of living that countless of our fellow citizens and even we would be loath to give up. Are we, for example, really willing to do without the wood that gives us home-building materials, furniture, fireplace fuel, and the pages in our books and newspapers? Are we willing to endure the increased prices of wood products that a reduced supply of timber would bring, increased prices that would inhibit a growing number of lower- and middle-income Americans from affording a home?

So the question is: How can the nation's environmentalist views and those of the conservationists and commercial interests be blended into a compromise that is satisfying to both sides?

This is a question all of us must face and attempt to answer. If each of us can arrive at an answer, we might be able to help resolve the conflict or be able to foster wise ideas and attitudes that will lead to that needed compromise.

Without the answer, we can be certain of one thing. We will be powerless to help and the American wilderness will remain a battleground for years to come.

SOURCE NOTES

CHAPTER ONE: THE BATTLEGROUND

1. W. Prochnau, "Last Stand for the Old Woods," *Life,* May 1990, 55–56.
2. The material on the National Park System is developed from *The National Parks: Index 1989,* U.S. Department of the Interior, 1989, 6–8, 13, 82.
3. The material on the National Forest System is developed from *Land Areas of the National Forest System, as of September 30, 1989,* U.S. Department of Agriculture (USDA), 1989, 2–3; *Report of the Forest Service: Fiscal Year 1989,* USDA, February 1990, 9, 14, 20, 33; *A Guide to Your National Forests* (a map and brochure), USDA, undated; *What the Forest Service Does,* USDA, October 1986, 6, 10, 12.
4. The material on the U.S. Bureau of Land Management is developed from M. Satchell, "The Battle for the Wilderness," *U.S. News & World Report,* July 3, 1989, 17–18.
5. The material on the Wilderness Areas is developed from P. Shabecoff, "A Rising Impulse to Leave the Land Alone," *New York Times,* June 11, 1989; Satchell, "Battle for the Wilderness," 20; *Report of the Forest Service,* 38.

CHAPTER TWO: OUR NATIONAL PARKS: THEIR STORY

1. The material on the founding of the Yellowstone National Park is developed from W. Stegner, "It All Began with Conservation," *Smithsonian Magazine,* April 1990, 40; *The National Parks: Index 1989,* U.S. Department of the Interior, 1989, 6, 82.
2. The material on John Muir and his role in the development of the National Park System is developed from E. F. Dolan, *Famous Builders of California* (New York: Dodd, Mead, 1987), 84–101; Stegner, "Conservation," 41; "Sequoia Celebrates 100 Years as Park," *San Francisco Chronicle,* August 20, 1990; *National Parks: Index 1989,* 18, 21, 22, 26, 79.
3. The material on the Antiquities Act of 1906 is developed from Stegner, "Conservation," 40.
4. The material on the National Park Act of 1916 is developed from Stegner, "Conservation," 40–41; *National Parks: Index 1989,* 6.

CHAPTER THREE: OUR THREATENED NATIONAL PARKS

1. The material on the increasing number of visitors to national parks and the reasons for the increase is developed from M. Hinds, "Anxious Armies of Vacationers Are Demanding More from Nature," *New York Times,* July 8, 1990.
2. The material in the section "An Odd Battleground" is developed from "Parks in Peril," *USA Today,* June 15, 1990.
3. The material in the section "Adding to the Strain" is developed from Hinds, "Anxious Armies of Vacationers"; "Parks in Peril"; *The National Parks: Index 1989,* U.S. Department of the Interior, 1989, 23.
4. The material on accommodations that must be built for park visitors is developed from: M. Goodage, "Officials Try to Balance Nature, Man," *USA Today,* June 15, 1990; E. Brazil, "Yosemite Lovers Not Fond of Change," *San Francisco Examiner,* January 21, 1990; A. Temko, "A New Vision Is Needed for Yosemite," *San Francisco Chronicle,* October 1, 1990.
5. The material on state and local parks is developed from Hinds, "Anxious Armies of Vacationers."
6. The material in the sections "Nontourist Damage: Inside

the Facilities" and "Nontourist Damage: From the Outside" is developed from M. Lemonick, "Invasion of the Habitat Snatchers," *Time,* September 10, 1990, 75; S. Mydons, "Grand Canyon's Air Is Being Polluted on 2 Fronts," *New York Times,* October 15, 1989; M. Satchell, "The Battle for the Wilderness," *U.S. News & World Report,* July 3, 1989, 19–20; "Parks in Peril."

7. Hinds, "Anxious Armies of Vacationers."

CHAPTER FOUR: MEETING THE THREATS

1. The material on what is being done about park overcrowding at the federal and state level is developed from M. Hinds, "Anxious Armies of Vacationers Are Demanding More from Nature," *New York Times,* July 8, 1990; M. Goodavage, "Officials Try to Balance Nature, Man," *USA Today,* June 15, 1990.
2. The material in all sections entitled "What You Can Do to Help" is developed from the author's personal experience and conversations with park officials over the years.
3. The material on what can be done to help vacationers get the most out of their park visits is developed from Hinds, "Anxious Armies of Vacationers."
4. The material on preserving a park's beauty and the plans for improving Sequoia and Yosemite National parks is developed from: Goodavage, "Officials Try to Balance Nature"; Hinds, "Anxious Armies of Vacationers"; C. Nolte, "Sequoia Park Tourist Buildings Will Soon Be Out of the Woods," *San Francisco Chronicle,* August 20, 1990; Nolte, "Yosemite Is 100—and Ailing," *San Francisco Chronicle,* September 28, 1990; A. Temko, "A New Vision Is Needed for Yosemite," *San Francisco Chronicle,* October 1, 1990; E. Diringer, "Flap Over Concession Deal," *San Francisco Chronicle*, September 25, 1991.
5. The material on the future control of exotic species is developed from *Policies of The Wildlife Society: A Stand on Issues Important to Wildlife Conservation* (Bethesda, Md.: The Wildlife Society, 1990), 2, 10.

CHAPTER FIVE: OF WETLANDS, LAKES, RIVERS, AND COASTS

1. The material on the harms being done to the Everglades National Park and the Florida Everglades is developed from J. Kass, "Florida's Great Everglades Is Dying a Little Each Year," *San Francisco Examiner* (from the *Chicago Tribune*), October 21, 1990; J. Schmalz, "Pollution-Fed Plants Choking Everglades," *San Francisco Chronicle* (from *New York Times*), September 18, 1989; *The National Parks: Index 1989*, U.S. Department of the Interior, 1989, 35.
2. The material on the damages seen in the Kesterson and Stillwater Wildlife refuges and other wetland regions is developed from J. Adler, "Troubled Waters," *Newsweek*, April 16, 1990, 71; R. Fitzgerald, "The Case of the Poisoned Wildlife Refuge," *Reader's Digest*, October 1987, 133, 137.
3. The material on acid rain is developed from E.F. Dolan, *Our Poisoned Sky* (New York, Cobblehill Books, Dutton, 1991), 39–40, 43, 48–55; J. Farrell, "Acid Rain: The Fallacies and the Facts," *San Francisco Examiner*, July 2, 1988; K. Schneider, "Lawmakers Reach an Accord on Reduction of Air Pollution," *New York Times*, October 23, 1990; P. Shabecoff, "An Emergence of Political Will on Acid Rain," *New York Times*, February 19, 1989; "The Environment's Gains and Losses," *New York Times*, December 4, 1988; "House OKs Clean Air Act—Bush Approval Expected," *San Francisco Chronicle*, October 27, 1990.
4. The material on the dangers to the Columbia, Snake, and Mississippi rivers and other waterways is developed from Adler, "Troubled Waters," 67, 70, 71, 80; J. Simson, "On Columbia, Fight Is Over Wild Salmon," *San Francisco Examiner* (from the *Seattle Times*), July 29, 1990; "17,365 Waterways Polluted, EPA Says," *San Francisco Chronicle*, June 14, 1989.
5. The material on the harms being done to the coasts is developed from: R. Diamond, "Tourists Avoiding New Jersey Like Plague," *San Francisco Examiner*, August 14, 1988; A. Toufexis, "The Dirty Sea," *Time*, August 1, 1988, 44–50; B. Workman, "Call for Bigger Marine Refuge," *San Francisco Chronicle*, August 24, 1990.

CHAPTER SIX: OUR NATIONAL FORESTS: THEIR STORY

1. The material on the two ideas that led to the unrestrained felling of the American forests by the early settlers is developed from W. Stegner, "It All Began with Conservation," *Smithsonian Magazine,* April 1990, 35, 38–39; "A Few Particulars, Part I," a section in the feature article by R. Rosenblatt, "Trees Were Invented to Contain and Reveal Secrets," *Life,* May 1990, 31.
2. The material on George Perkins Marsh is developed from Stegner, "Conservation," 38; R. Nelson, "Mythology Instead of Analysis," a chapter in the book *Forestlands: Public and Private* (San Diego: Pacific Institute for Public Policy Research, 1985), 26.
3. The material on the influence of Marsh's work on conservationists and political leaders is developed from Stegner, "Conservation," 38–39; Nelson, "Mythology," 26–27; "Celebrating 100 Years of the National Forest System," *Beginnings: Newsletter for the 1991 National Forest System Centennial,* U.S. Department of Agriculture, dated 1989, 1, 4.
4. The material on the first national forests is developed from: Stegner, 39; Nelson, 27–29; E. F. Dolan, *Famous Builders of California* (New York: Dodd, Mead, 1987), 97–98; P. Shabecoff, "The Battle for the National Forests," *New York Times,* August 13, 1989; Rosenblatt, "Trees Were Invented," 54.
5. The material on Gifford Pinchot's philosophy of forest management and utilization is developed from Nelson, "Mythology," 29–30.

CHAPTER SEVEN: THE FOREST CONFLICT

1. The material on the amount of cutting that has been done and is currently being done in the national forests is developed from W. Brookes, "Forest Defenders Have Gone Overboard," *San Francisco Chronicle,* April 20, 1990; R. Nelson, "Mythology Instead of Analysis," a chapter in the book *Forestlands: Public and Private* (San Diego: Pacific Institute of Public Policy Research, 1985), 48, 49; P. Sha-

becoff, "The Battle for the National Forests," *New York Times,* August 13, 1989; *Report of the Forest Service: Fiscal Year 1989,* U.S. Department of Agriculture (USDA), February 1990, 27–28; *What the Forest Service Does,* USDA, October 1986, 10–12.

2. The material on clear-cutting is developed from R. Findley, "Will We Save Our Own?" *National Geographic,* September 1990, 112; H. Gilliam, "The Long and Winding Ballot," *This World Magazine, San Francisco Chronicle,* October 7, 1990, 18; J. Kay, "The Last Stand," *Image Magazine, San Francisco Chronicle,* August 26, 1990, 21; M. Hoffman, ed., *The World Almanac and Book of Facts 1990* (New York: Pharos Books, 1990), 216.
3. The material on the greenhouse effect is developed from: R. Bidinotto, "What Is the Truth About Global Warming?" *Reader's Digest,* February 1990, 93–97; J. Brooke, "Amazon City Tastes of Wood Smoke," *New York Times,* August 5, 1990; L. Brown, project director, *State of the World, 1989: A Worldwatch Institute Report on Progress Toward a Sustainable Society* (New York: W. W. Norton, 1989), 4, 26, 29, 31; J. Christensen, "Plan to Tap Oil in Ecuador Enrages Environmentalists," *San Francisco Chronicle* (Pacific News Service report), October 9, 1990; E. F. Dolan, *Our Poisoned Sky* (New York: Cobblehill Books, Dutton, 1990), 56–60, 64–65; E. F. Dolan, *Drought: The Past, Present, and Future Enemy* (New York: Franklin Watts, 1990), 111–18; P. Smucker, "Southeast Asia Devours Its Rain Forests," *San Francisco Examiner,* July 15, 1990; W. Stevens, "Culprit in the Greenhouse Effect," *San Francisco Chronicle* (from the *New York Times*), November 29, 1989.
4. The material on the cutting of the old-growth forests is developed from: W. Brookes; M. Lemonick, "Showdown in the Treetops," *Time,* August 28, 1989, 58–59; W. Prochnau, "Last Stand for the Old Woods," *Life,* May 1990, 54–55; Shabecoff, "Battle for the National Forests."
5. The material on the cutting of the old-growth forests in British Columbia, Canada, is developed from T. Egan, "Struggles Over the Ancient Trees Shift to British Columbia," *New York Times,* April 15, 1990.

CHAPTER EIGHT: THE BATTLE OVER THE OLD-GROWTH FORESTS

1. The material on the activist organization, Earth First, is developed from E. Diringer, "Environmental Group Says It Won't Spike Trees," *San Francisco Chronicle*, April 11, 1990; B. Israel, "Tense Logging Protest Caps Redwood Summer," *San Francisco Chronicle*, September 4, 1990; M. Lemonick, "Showdown in the Treetops," *Time*, August 28, 1989, 58, 59; "Environmentalists in Bombing," *Facts on File*, June 1, 1990, 406.
2. The material on the Libby, Montana, agreement is developed from D. Baum, "Burying the Ax: Peace Pact in a Logging War," *San Francisco Examiner*, August 5, 1990.
3. The material on the northern spotted owl and its placement on the Endangered Species List is developed from E. Diringer, "White House Blasted Over Owl, Logging," *San Francisco Chronicle*, September 22, 1990; M. Fischer, "The Ancient Forests Are Falling," *Sierra*, March/April 1990, 6; T. Gup, "Owl vs. Man," *Time*, June 25, 1990, 57, 59, 60; Lemonick, "Showdown," 59; M. Satchell, "The Endangered Logger," *U.S. News & World Report*, June 25, 1990, 27, 28; "Owls Need Lots More Timber, Scientists Inform Congress," *San Francisco Chronicle* (from the *Los Angeles Times*), April 5, 1990; "Scientists Back Logging Ban," *Facts on File*, June 1, 1990, 406; "Spotted Owl: Still in Danger," *Time*, July 2, 1990, 27; "No Peace for the Owl," *Time*, July 9, 1990, 63.
4. The material on the 1990 election measures in California and the public reactions they triggered is developed from: R. Lacayo, "No Lack of Initiatives: California Debates a Thicket of Environmental Proposals," *Time*, September 3, 1990, 52; W. Prochnau, "Last Stand for the Old Woods," *Life*, May 1990, 55; Satchell, "Endangered Logger," 28.

CHAPTER NINE: OUR WILDERNESS AREAS: THE NEWEST BATTLEGROUND

1. The material on the wilderness areas is developed from M. Satchell, "The Battle for the Wilderness," *U.S. News & World Report*, July 3, 1989, 16–21; *The National Parks: Index 1989*, U.S. Department of the Interior, 1989, 8;

Report of the Forest Service: Fiscal Year 1989, U.S. Department of Agriculture (USDA), 1990, 38; *What the Forest Service Does,* USDA, 1986, 12–13.

2. The material on the Wilderness Act is developed from: P. Shabecoff, "A Rising American Impulse to Leave the Land Alone," *New York Times,* June 11, 1989; "An Act to Establish a National Wilderness Preservation System for the Permanent Good of the Whole People, and for Other Purposes," U.S. Senate and House of Representatives, September 3, 1963.
3. The material in the section "A New Battleground" is developed from: D. Baum, "New Coalition Declares Open Season on Public Land," *San Francisco Examiner,* July 22, 1990; Satchell, "Battle for the Wilderness," 16–21; the offices of Senator Alan Cranston (California), Congresspersons Barbara Boxer (California), Wayne Owens (Utah), and Barbara Vucanovich (Nevada); information supplied by the U.S. Bureau of Land Management, California State Office.

BIBLIOGRAPHY

BOOKS AND BOOKLETS

Bowen, Ezra, and the Editors of Time-Life Books. *The High Sierra*. New York: Time-Life Books, 1972.

Brown, Lester R., project director. *State of the World, 1989: A Worldwatch Institute Report on Progress Toward a Sustainable Society*. New York: W. W. Norton, 1989.

———. *State of the World, 1990: A Worldwatch Institute Report on Progress Toward a Sustainable Society*. New York: W. W. Norton, 1990.

Conservation Policies of The Wildlife Society. Bethesda, Md.: The Wildlife Society, 1990.

Dolan, Edward F. *Famous Builders of California*. New York: Dodd, Mead, 1987.

———. *Drought: The Past, Present, and Future Enemy*. New York: Franklin Watts, 1990.

———. *Our Poisoned Sky*. New York: Cobblehill Books, Dutton, 1991.

Farb, Peter, and the Editors of Time-Life Books. *Ecology*. New York: Time-Life Books, 1963, 1970.

Hardy, Ralph; Wright, Peter; Kington, John; and Gribbin, John. *The Weather Book*. Boston: Little, Brown, 1982.

McKibben, Bill. *The End of Nature*. New York: Random House, 1989.

Steger, Will, and Bowermaster, Jon. *Saving the Earth: A Citizen's Guide to Environmental Action*. New York: Knopf, 1990.

Weiner, Jonathan. *Planet Earth*. New York: Bantam Books, 1986.

MAGAZINES

Adler, Jerry. "Troubled Waters." *Newsweek,* April 16, 1990.

Bidinotto, Robert James. "What Is the Truth About Global Warming?" *Reader's Digest,* February 1990.

Chowder, Ken. "Can We Afford the Wilderness?" *Modern Maturity,* June–July 1990.

Easterbrook, George. "Try to Follow the Pea." *Newsweek,* February 19, 1990.

Facts on File. "Scientists Back Logging Ban," June 1, 1990.

Findley, Rowe. "Will We Save Our Own?" *National Geographic,* September 1990.

Fischer, Michael L. "The Ancient Forests Are Falling," *Sierra,* March/April 1990.

Fitzgerald, Randy. "The Case of the Poisoned Wildlife Refuge." *Reader's Digest,* October 1987.

Gilliam, Harold. "Logging: Not a Clear-Cut Case." *This World Magazine, San Francisco Chronicle,* September 2, 1990.

———. "The Long and Winding Ballot." *This World Magazine, San Francisco Chronicle,* October 7, 1990.

Gup, Ted. "Owl vs. Man." *Time,* June 25, 1990.

Howard, Beth, and Berger, Bob. "Lost Horizons." *Omni,* September 1990.

Kay, Jane. "The Last Stand." *Image Magazine, San Francisco Chronicle,* August 26, 1990.

Lacayo, Richard. "No Lack of Initiatives: California Debates a Thicket of Environmental Proposals." *Time,* September 3, 1990.

Laycock, George. "What Water for Stillwater?" *Audubon,* November 1988.

Lemonick, Michael D. "Showdown in the Treetops." *Time,* August 28, 1989.

———. "Invasion of the Habitat Snatchers." *Time,* September 10, 1990.

Mitchell, John G. "War in the Woods." *Audubon,* January 1990.

Prochnau, William. "Last Stand for the Old Woods." *Life,* May 1990.

Rice, Odell. "Conservation in the Bush Era." *American Forests,* May–June 1989.

Satchell, Michael. "The Battle for the Wilderness." *U.S. News & World Report,* July 3, 1989.

———. "The Endangered Logger." *U.S. News & World Report,* June 25, 1990.

Time. "Still at Loggerheads," July 10, 1989.

———. "Environment's Little Big Bird," April 16, 1990.

———. "Spotted Owl: Still in Danger," July 2, 1990.

———. "No Peace for the Owl," July 9, 1990.

Toufexis, Anastasia. "The Dirty Seas." *Time,* August 1, 1988.

Spencer, Cathy. "Frogs and Other Amphibians Are Telling Us Something About Our Environment—They're Croaking." *Omni,* October 1990.

Stegner, Wallace. "It All Began with Conservation," *Smithsonian Magazine,* April 1990.

NEWSPAPERS

Baum, Dan. "New Coalition Declares Open Season on Public Land." *San Francisco Examiner,* July 22, 1990.

———. "Burying the Ax: Peace Pact in a Logging War." *San Francisco Examiner,* August 5, 1990.

Brazil, Eric. "Yosemite Lovers Not Fond of Change." *San Francisco Examiner,* January 21, 1990.

Diamond, Randy. "Tourists Avoiding Jersey Like Plague." *San Francisco Examiner,* August 14, 1988.

Diringer, Elliot. "Environmentalists Win a Round in Battle for Old-Growth Forests." *San Francisco Chronicle,* April 6, 1990.

———. "Environmental Group Says It Won't Spike Trees." *San Francisco Chronicle,* April 11, 1990.

———. "White House Blasted Over Owl, Logging," *San Francisco Chronicle,* September 22, 1990.

Egan, Timothy. "Struggles Over the Ancient Trees Shift to British Columbia." *New York Times,* April 15, 1990.

———. "In West, a Showdown Over Rules on Grazing." *New York Times,* August 19, 1990.

Gold, Allan R. "Northeast Forests, Too, Get Congress's Attention." *New York Times,* October 29, 1989.

Goodage, Maria. "Officials Try to Balance Nature, Man." *USA Today,* June 15, 1990.

Gross, Jane. "A Treetop Only Wings and Hopes Can Touch." *New York Times,* December 24, 1989.

Hinds, Michael deCourcy. "Anxious Armies of Vacationers Are Demanding More from Nature." *New York Times,* July 8, 1990.

Israel, Bill. "Tense Logging Protest Caps Redwood Summer." *San Francisco Chronicle,* September 4, 1990.

Kass, John. "Florida's Great Everglades Is Dying a Little Each Year." *San Francisco Examiner* (from *Chicago Tribune*), October 21, 1990.

Los Angeles Times, "Grand Canyon Haze Blamed on Power Plant," October 6, 1990.

Mydons, Seth. "Grand Canyon's Air Is Being Polluted on 2 Fronts." *New York Times,* October 15, 1989.

New York Times. "The Environment's Gains and Losses." December 4, 1988.

Nolte, Carl. "Sequoia Park Tourist Buildings Will Be Out of the Woods." *San Francisco Chronicle,* August 20, 1990.

———. "Group to Challenge Profits at Yosemite." *San Francisco Chronicle,* September 20, 1990.

———. "Yosemite Is 100—and Ailing." *San Francisco Chronicle,* September 28, 1990.

———. "House OKs Clean Air Act—Bush Approval Expected." *San Francisco Chronicle,* October 27, 1990.

Perlman, David. "Heavy Lead Pollution Found in Sea Otters." *San Francisco Chronicle,* October 11, 1990.

Reinhold, Robert. "At Yosemite, Environmentalists Compete with Entrepreneurs for Business." *New York Times,* September 23, 1990.

Robbins, Jim. "A New Kind of Mining Disaster." *New York Times,* February 5, 1989.

San Francisco Chronicle. "17,365 Waterways Polluted, EPA Says," June 14, 1989.

———. "Owls Need Lots More Timber, Scientists Inform Congress" (from *Los Angeles Times*), April 5, 1990.

———. "Owl Study Reportedly Suppressed" (from Associated Press), July 20, 1990.

———. "New Rules on Owl Stump Loggers," September 7, 1990.

San Francisco Examiner. "Loggers, Activists Square Off," July 22, 1990.

———. "Environmental Issues on November Ballot," September 23, 1990.

Schmalz, Jeffrey. "Pollution-Fed Plants Choking Everglades." *San Francisco Chronicle* (from *New York Times*), September 18, 1989.

Schneider, Keith. "Lawmakers Reach an Accord on Reduction of Air Pollution." *New York Times,* October 23, 1990.

Shabecoff, Philip. "An Emergence of Political Will on Acid Rain." *New York Times,* February 19, 1989.

———. "A Rising American Impulse to Leave the Land Alone." *New York Times,* June 11, 1989.

———. "The Battle for the National Forests." *New York Times,* August 13, 1989.

Simson, Jim. "On Columbia, Fight Is Over Wild Salmon." *San Francisco Examiner* (from the *Seattle Times*), July 29, 1990.

Smucker, Phillip. "Southeast Asia Devours Its Rain Forests." *San Francisco Examiner,* July 15, 1990.

Stevens, William K. "Culprit in the Greenhouse Effect," *San Francisco Chronicle* (from *New York Times*), November 29, 1989.

Sylvester, David A. "New Logging Rules to Help Spotted Owl." *San Francisco Chronicle,* July 12, 1990.

Temko, Allan. "A New Vision Is Needed for Yosemite." *San Francisco Chronicle,* October 1, 1990.

USA Today. "Parks in Peril," June 15, 1990.

Verhovek, Sam Howe. "The Latest Plan for the Adirondacks Leaves Adirondackers Skeptical." *New York Times,* June 10, 1990.

Workman, Bill. "Call for Bigger Marine Refuge." *San Francisco Chronicle,* August 24, 1990.

GOVERNMENT PUBLICATIONS

From the U.S. Department of the Interior, Washington, D.C.:

Management Policies: U.S. Department of Interior National Park Service, 1988. 1988.

The National Parks: Index 1989. 1989.

From the Department of Agriculture, Washington, D.C.:

What the Forest Service Does. 1986.

Land Areas of the National Forest System, As of September 30, 1989. 1989.

Report of the Forest Service: Fiscal Year 1989. 1990.

National Forests: 1891–1991. No publication date given.

"An Act to Establish a National Wilderness Preservation System for the Permanent Good of the Whole People, and for Other Purposes." United States Congress, enacted 1963.

TELEVISION TRANSCRIPTS

"The Greenhouse Effect." *Nightline*, American Broadcasting Company, September 7, 1988.

INDEX